COMPAN TRAVEL GUIDE TO

ITHACA, GREECE

Must See, Must Do Activities! Top Attractions! Insider and Local Tips! Cultural Immersion!

CARL DIAZ

COPYRIGHT NOTICE

This publication is copyright-protected. This is only for personal use. No part of this publication may be, reproduced, in any form or medium, stored in a data retrieval system or transmitted by or through any means, without prior written permission from the Author.

Legal action will be pursued if this is breached.

SCAN HERE TO GAIN ACCESS TO ALL MY BOOKS

DISCLAIMER

Please note that the information contained within this document s for educational purposes only. The information contained herein has been obtained from sources believed to be reliable at the time of publication. The opinions expressed herein are subject to change without notice. Readers acknow edge that the Author / Publisher is not engaging in rendering legal, financial or professional advice.

In addition, I cisclaim all warranties as to the accuracy, completeness, or adequacy of such information. Also, note that the paperback is black and white, I understand that it is not ideal but so as to reduce cost; however, if you want a colored version, kindly check out the kindle version, it has full colored maps and images that you can zoom in, which is quite helpful.

Lastly, this guide is meant to give you all the basic info you need quickly, a shortcut to aid your planning without spending a lot of time online, so remember that this is just a starting point as there's always more to discover on your own. Thank you for choosing this city's guide, I hope it makes your journey memorable and easier.

Table of Contents

- DISCLAIMER 3
- INTRODUCTION 11
  - Welcome to Ithaca 11
  - Why should I visit Ithaca? 12
  - Brief History and Cultural Background 12
    - Cultural Heritage 16
- Chapter 1 21
- GETTING THERE 21
  - By Air: Nearest Airports 21
  - By Sea: Ferries to Ithaca 22
  - By Road 24
  - Travel Tips and Recommendations 25
  - Visa and entry requirements 26
    - Visa Requirements for Ithaca, Greece 26
    - Entry Requirements: 30
- Chapter 2 33
- BEST TIME TO VISIT AND DURATION OF STAY 33
  - Seasonal Highlights 33
  - Ideal Duration for Different Types of Travelers 35
- Chapter 3 40
- TOP TOURIST ATTRACTIONS 40
  - Vathy: The Charming Capital 40
    - Exploring Vathy 41

- Dining and Shopping in Vathy 43
- Historic Sites 44
- Activities and Leisure 45
- Events & Festivals 46
- Practical Information 47

Kioni: A Picturesque Village 48
- Village Overview 49
- Practical Tips for Visiting Kioni. 54

Stavros: Heart of Northern Ithaca 55
- Practical Tips for Visiting Stavros 62

Anogi: Ancient Ruins and Monastery 63
- Monastery of Panagia Eleousa 63
- Menir: The Ancient Standing Stones 64
- The village of Anogi 66
- Practical information 67

Filiatro Beach: A Beach Paradise 68

Gidaki Beach: Secluded Beauty 72
- Getting to Gidaki Beach 73
- Beach Highlights: 74
- Practical information 75
- Nearby Attractions 77

The Archaeological Site of Alalcomenae: Historical Insights 78
- What to Expect 79

- Practical Information 80
- Nearby Attractions 81
- Highlights 82
- Aetos: Ancient Ruins and Modern Views 83
  - Highlights of the Mycenaean Site 84
  - Practical information 86
  - Nearby Attractions 88
- Lazaretto Islet: Historical Landmark 89
  - Highlights of Lazaretto Islet 90
  - Practical Information 92

Chapter 4 94
ITINERARIES FOR DIFFERENT TRAVELERS 94
- Weekend Getaway 94
  - Day 1: Arrival and Initial Exploration 94
  - Day 2: Adventure and Relaxation 95
- Cultural Immersion 95
  - Day 1: Historical Insights 95
  - Day 2: Local Traditions and Cuisine 96
- Outdoor Adventure 97
  - Day 1: Hiking and Scenic Views 97
  - Day 2: Water Adventures 98
- Family-Friendly Trip 98
  - Day 1: Interactive Exploration 98
  - Day 2: Fun and Learning 99

- Budget Travel 100
  - Day 1: Economical Exploration 100
  - Day 2: Affordable Adventures 101
- Solo Traveler's Guide 101
  - Day 1: Solo Exploration 101
  - Day 2: Personal Adventure 102
- Romantic Getaways 103
  - Day 1: Romantic Scenery 103
  - Day 2: Love and Adventure 104

Chapter 5 105
PRACTICAL TIPS 105
- Health and Safety Precautions 105
- Communication and Language Tips 106
- Local Etiquette and Customs 107

Chapter 6 109
TRANSPORTATION WITHIN ITHACA 109
- Public Transport Options 109
- Car Rental and Driving Tips 110
- Biking and Walking Routes 112
- Boat Rentals and Water Taxi 113

Chapter 7 115
LOCAL EXPLORATION AND ADVENTURE 115
- Hiking Trails and Nature Walks 115
- Sailing and Boating Adventures 117

- Snorkeling and diving spots 118
- Local Tours and Guided Excursions 120
- Practical Tips for Exploration 121

Chapter 8 124
BUDGETING AND MONETARY TIPS 124
- Daily Expense Estimates 124
- Money Saving Tips 125
- Currency Exchange and Banking Services 127
- Shopping and Bargaining 128

Chapter 9 130
SHOPPING AND ENTERTAINMENT IN ITHACA 130
- Local markets and souvenir shops 130
- Art galleries and cultural centers 132
- Evening Entertainment & Events 133
- Shopping and Entertainment Tips: 135

Chapter 10 137
DINING AND NIGHTLIFE 137
- Traditional Greek cuisine 137
- Top Restaurants and Cafes 139
- Popular Bars and Nightclubs 140
- Local Food Festivals & Events 142

Chapter 11 145
ACCOMMODATION OPTIONS 145
- Luxury resorts 145

Budget-Friendly Hotels 146

　　Boutique guesthouses 148

　　Unique Stays 149

　　Top Recommended Accommodation 150

　　Choosing the Right Accommodation for You 151

　　Booking Tips and Tricks 152

　　Booking Platforms 153

Chapter 12 155

WHAT TO DO AND NOT TO DO 155

　　Respecting Local Culture 155

　　Environmental considerations 156

　　Safety Tips for Tourists 158

CONCLUSION AND FAREWELL 160

APPENDIX: USEFUL RESOURCES 162

　　Emergency Contacts and Contact Information 162

　　Maps and Navigational Tools 164

　　Additional Reading and References 165

　　Useful Local Phrases 166

　　Addresses and Locations of Popular Accommodation 170

　　Addresses and Locations of Popular Restaurants and Cafes 171

　　Addresses and Locations of Popular Bars and Clubs .. 172

　　Addresses and Locations of Book Shops 173

Addresses and Locations of Top Clinics, Hospitals, and Pharmacies 174
Addresses and Locations of UNESCO World Heritage Sites 175
Photo or image attribution 175
MAPS 178

INTRODUCTION

Welcome to Ithaca

Ithaca! Just saying the name evokes a sense of adventure and a journey well worth taking. This lovely island in the Ionian Sea, just off the coast of mainland Greece, appears to have stepped straight out of mythology. As a seasoned traveler and frequent visitor to Ithaca, I can assure you that there is no place quite like it. The island is rich in history, natural beauty, and a warm, friendly attitude that immediately makes you feel at home.

Why should I visit Ithaca?

You might question why Ithaca. What distinguishes this island from the many other gorgeous Greek destinations? For me, it's the ideal combination of tranquil landscapes, rich history, and vibrant local culture. Ithaca is more than just a destination; it's an experience. It's the type of place where you can lose yourself in nature's beauty while also delving into old history and immersing yourself in the local way of life.

Ithaca has something for everyone, whether you want to relax, go on an adventure, or learn about a new culture. From the crystal-clear waters of its secluded beaches to the quaint beauty of its communities, every aspect of the island has a tale. And don't forget about the welcoming people who are always willing to share their stories and traditions with guests.

Brief History and Cultural Background

Ithaca is a place where history and myth intersect, resulting in a complex tapestry that has captivated researchers, tourists, and dreamers for millennia. The island's history begins in the mists of prehistory and continues through the Classical, Byzantine, and modern periods, with each leaving an indelible stamp on Ithaca's cultural environment.

Prehistoric and Mycenaean periods

Ithaca's history may be dated back to the Neolithic period, approximately 3000 BCE. Archaeological evidence reveals that the island was home to early people who conducted agriculture and animal husbandry. Ithaca rose to prominence during the Mycenaean period (between 1600 and 1100 BCE).

The Mycenaean civilization, known for its advanced architecture, art, and trade, established a significant presence on Ithaca. The island is popularly associated with the mythological king Odysseus, the hero of Homer's epic poem the Odyssey. According to the epic, Odysseus was the king of Ithaca, and his long, perilous trip home from the Trojan War is a prominent element. While the Odyssey's historical veracity is debatable, the myth has solidified Ithaca's place in literary history.

Significant Mycenaean items, including pottery, tools, and structural ruins, have been discovered during excavations in the Stavros area, indicating that Ithaca was an important center during this time period. The so-called "Palace of Odysseus," whose exact location is unknown, continues to pique people's interest and inspire inquiry.

Classic and Hellenistic Periods

Following the decline of the Mycenaean civilization, Ithaca fell into relative obscurity. Ithaca did not regain prominence until the Classical period (approximately 5th-4th centuries BCE). The island was part of the Corinthian area of influence, which eventually became the Athenian Alliance.

During this time, Ithaca established its own political and social systems, becoming a minor but active player in the larger Greek world. The remnants of old acropolises and other fortifications from this time period can still be seen on the island, providing insight into its strategic significance and defensive capabilities.

The Hellenistic period (circa 323-31 BCE) brought further development and prosperity to Ithaca. The island grew more interwoven into the larger Hellenistic world, resulting in increased trade and cultural exchange. Archaeologists have found some of the key public buildings and infrastructure built during this era.

Roman and Byzantine periods

Ithaca fell under Roman rule in the second century BCE, following the Roman invasion of Greece. The island's strategic location makes it a vital stop on nautical routes in the Ionian Sea. Under Roman administration, Ithaca was relatively stable and prosperous, with increased agricultural production and trade.

Ithaca was incorporated into the Byzantine Empire after the Western Roman Empire collapsed. The Byzantine period (approximately 4th-15th centuries CE) saw the construction of several significant ecclesiastical and military facilities. Churches, monasteries, and strongholds were built, and many of them are still significant cultural and historical sites today.

Venetian and Ottoman periods

The Republic of Venice took control of Ithaca in the late Middle Ages. The Venetians dominated Ithaca from the 16th to the late 18th centuries, leaving an indelible mark on the island's architecture, culture, and society. The Venetian period was marked by relative peace and prosperity, with the construction of impressive palaces, fortresses, and the expansion of trading networks.

Following Napoleon's defeat of Venice, Ithaca briefly became French territory before being returned to the British in the early nineteenth century. During this time, the island underwent substantial social and economic developments, such as the establishment of schools and the adoption of contemporary administrative procedures.

Modern era

Ithaca and the neighboring Ionian islands joined the Kingdom of Greece in 1864. The island's contemporary history has been impacted by larger events in Greek history, such as the war for independence, the Balkan Wars, World War II, and the ensuing Greek Civil War.

Ithaca experienced modernization and development during the 20th century, including advances in infrastructure, education, and healthcare. Despite these changes, Ithaca has maintained its historic character and charm, creating a one-of-a-kind blend of the old and new.

Cultural Heritage

Ithaca's cultural heritage is a rich tapestry woven from various historical influences. The island's culture is defined by a strong sense of community, a rich storytelling history, and a deep connection to the water.

Festivals and Traditions

Ithacans celebrate various festivals throughout the year, many of which are based on ancient customs. The most notable of these is the Feast of Panagia, which takes place in mid-August and commemorates the Assumption of the Virgin Mary. The celebration features religious processions, traditional music, dancing, and eating, giving guests a chance to learn about local customs and hospitality.

Other significant events include the Carnival of Vathy, which features colorful parades and exuberant celebrations, and the Feast of St. Nicholas, the patron saint of sailors, which honors the island's maritime tradition.

Music & Dance

Music and dance are integral parts of Ithacan culture. Traditional Greek music, with its unique melodies and rhythms, can be heard during festivals, taverns, and family gatherings. The island's folk dances, which are frequently accompanied by live music, are enjoyable to observe and engage in. Popular dances include the Kalamatianos, Sirtaki, and the boisterous Hasapiko.

Cuisine

Ithacan cuisine is a delectable blend of the island's agricultural richness and nautical influences. Fresh fish, locally grown veggies, and olive oil are essential components of the diet. Sofrito (a veal dish with white wine and garlic), bourdetto (a spicy fish stew), and kreatopita (a savory meat pie) are some of the traditional foods. The island's honey and native cheeses are also highly valued.

Dining in Ithaca is about the experience as much as the food. Meals are typically leisurely occasions, shared with family and friends and accompanied by local wine or ouzo. Tavernas and eateries throughout the island provide an opportunity to experience authentic Greek flavors while experiencing the warm welcome of the inhabitants.

Handicraft and Art

Ithaca has a strong tradition of handicrafts and art. Local craftsmen create stunning pottery, textiles, and jewelry, frequently utilizing techniques passed down through generations. These crafts reflect the island's cultural past and offer unique keepsakes. Ithaca also features a burgeoning group of contemporary artists who are inspired by the island's natural beauty and rich history.

Living Traditions

Ithacans are proud of their cultural heritage and actively try to preserve it. This is obvious in how they celebrate their festivals, preserve their historical structures, and pass along their stories and rituals to future generations. As a guest, you'll have numerous possibilities to interact with this living heritage, such as attending a local festival, learning a traditional dance, or simply speaking with people.

Architectural Heritage

Ithaca's architecture is a mix of styles, representing the diverse cultures that have impacted the island over the years. Traditional homes with red-tiled roofs, Venetian-style structures, Byzantine cathedrals, and British-era administrative buildings all add to the island's distinct architectural landscape.

Notable architectural landmarks include the Church of Agios Nikolaos in Vathy, which has wonderful frescoes and iconostasis, and the medieval Monastery of Panagia Kathariotissa, which has breathtaking views of the island and the sea.

Natural Beauty and Environmental Conservation

Ithaca's natural beauty is one of its most valuable assets. The island's craggy shoreline, crystal-clear waters, lush green hills, and calm beaches make it a nature lover's paradise. Hiking routes run around the island, providing beautiful vistas and opportunity to explore its rich flora and animals.

The inhabitants of Ithaca are dedicated to protecting their natural environment. Conservation initiatives are aimed at safeguarding the island's distinctive ecosystems, keeping beaches and waters clean, and encouraging sustainable tourism practices. Visitors are invited to respect and support these efforts, ensuring that Ithaca's natural beauty be enjoyed for future generations.

Conclusion

This introduction only scratched the surface of what Ithaca has to offer. As we progress through this travel guide, I'll provide more information about the island's attractions, practical recommendations, itineraries, and much more, allowing you to make the most of your visit to this wonderful island.

Chapter 1
GETTING THERE

Whether you arrive by plane, sea, or road, this chapter will help you navigate your way to this magical island. To make your trip to Ithaca as seamless and comfortable as possible, we'll explore the greatest travel advice and recommendations. As someone who has spent a significant amount of time on this island, I am eager to share my experiences with you.

By Air: Nearest Airports

While Ithaca does not have its own airport, the nearest major airport is Kefalonia International Airport (EFL), which is on the adjacent island of Kefalonia. Kefalonia International Airport is well-connected to many locations in Europe, particularly during the summer. Major airlines such as Aegean Airlines, Ryanair, and EasyJet offer regular flights to Kefalonia from Athens, London, and Berlin.

Getting from Kefalonia to Ithaca

After arriving at Kefalonia International Airport, travel to the port of Sami to catch a ferry to Ithaca. The distance between the airport and Sami is roughly 34 kilometers (21 miles), and you can travel there by taxi or bus. The taxi travel takes about 45 minutes, and buses are available but infrequent. If you intend to use this route, I recommend that you check the bus timetable in advance.

Tips for air travel

- **Book Early:** Flights to Kefalonia can sell out quickly during high travel seasons, so book your tickets well in advance.
- **Travel Light:** Because you'll be transferring from an airport to a ferry, traveling light will make your trip more comfortable.
- **Stay updated:** Keep an eye on airline and boat schedules, as they may alter due to weather or other circumstances.

By Sea: Ferries to Ithaca

Ferries are the most common means to get to Ithaca, and they provide a lovely and pleasant ride across the Ionian Sea. There are multiple ferry routes to Ithaca that depart from several ports in Greece.

From Kefalonia.

The most direct route to Ithaca is via Sami on the island of Kefalonia. Ferries from Sami to Ithaca travel numerous times per day, with the journey taking approximately one hour and thirty minutes. The boat will arrive at Pisaetos or Vathy, depending on the service.

From Patras.

If you are coming from mainland Greece, you can take a ferry from the port of Patras. Patras is a large port in Greece that is well connected to the rest of the country. The boat voyage from Patras to Ithaca takes about 3 to 4 hours, making it an easy choice for travelers traveling from Athens or other mainland destinations.

From Lefkada.

Another option is to travel from the neighboring island of Lefkada. Ferries from Lefkada to Ithaca normally leave from the port of Nydri. The ride takes about 2 hours, and it's a terrific opportunity to explore two gorgeous Ionian islands.

Ferry Tips

- **Check Schedules:** Ferry schedules change depending on the season, so make sure to check the most recent timetables online or at the port.
- **Arrive Early:** To ensure a smooth boarding process, arrive at the port at least 30 minutes before the departure time.
- **Comfort Items**: Bring snacks, water, and entertainment for the ferry voyage, especially if the journey is long.

By Road

Driving to the Port

If you prefer to drive, you can get to the mainland ports of Patras or Killini and take a ferry to Ithaca from there. Both ports may be reached by vehicle from major cities such as Athens.

From Athens to Patras

The travel from Athens to Patras takes about 2.5 hours via the E94 and E65 highways. The road is well-maintained, and you will travel through some beautiful scenery along the way. Once at Patras, you can leave your car at the harbor and board the ferry to Ithaca.

From Athens to Killini

Alternatively, you can drive from Athens to Killini in around three hours using the E94 and E55 highways. Killini provides ferry connections to both Ithaca and Kefalonia, giving you more choice in your travel plans.

Road Trip Tips:

- **GPS Navigation:** To navigate the highways and prevent getting lost, use a reputable GPS or map app.
- **Rest Stops:** Make plans for rest stops along the trip, especially if you're traveling with children or need to take a break.
- **Fuel Up:** Make sure your vehicle has adequate fuel before you begin your journey, as petrol stations may be limited in some locations.

Travel Tips and Recommendations

Packing Essentials

When traveling to Ithaca, it is critical to pack wisely to guarantee a comfortable and pleasurable journey. Here are some items to consider bringing:

- **Lightweight Clothing:** Ithaca's climate is typically warm and sunny, so pack light, breathable clothing suitable for beach and outdoor activities.
- **Swimwear:** Remember to pack your swimsuit because you'll be spending a lot of time at Ithaca's lovely beaches.
- **Comfortable Footwear:** Bring comfortable walking shoes and sandals for the beach.
- **Sunscreen and Hat:** Use a wide-brimmed hat and high SPF sunscreen to protect yourself from the sun.
- **Travel adaptor:** If you are traveling from outside Europe, you will need a travel adaptor for your electronic equipment.

Visa and entry requirements

Visa Requirements for Ithaca, Greece

Before embarking on your journey to the gorgeous island of Ithaca, it is critical to understand the visa and entry requirements for Greece. Greece, being a member of the Schengen Area, has different entrance requirements based on your nationality.

Schengen Area Overview

Greece is a member of the Schengen Agreement, which provides passport-free travel between numerous European nations. The Schengen Area consists of 26 European countries that have removed internal borders, making it easy to travel between them. This agreement affects visa procedures for visitors visiting Greece, particularly Ithaca.

Entry for EU/EEA citizens

Citizens of the European Union (EU) and European Economic Area (EEA) nations do not require a visa to visit Greece. They can come to Ithaca and stay indefinitely with only a valid national ID card or passport. This includes travelers from Germany, France, Italy, and Sweden.

Entry for Non-EU/EEA Citizens

Visa rules differ for travelers from countries outside the EU and EEA. Below are the general guidelines for some common non-EU/EEA countries:

United States, Canada, Australia, and New Zealand

Citizens of the United States, Canada, Australia, and New Zealand are permitted to enter Greece without a visa for short periods of up to 90 days within a 180-day period for tourism or business. A valid passport is required for entrance and must be valid for at least three months after the desired stay.

United Kingdom

Post-Brexit, UK citizens can also enter Greece for short stays of up to 90 days within a 180-day period without a visa for tourism or business purposes. A valid passport is necessary, with at least three months validity beyond the anticipated stay.

Other Countries

Travelers from other countries should check the visa requirements particular to their nationality. Greece has agreements with various countries that allow for visa-free short stays. If your nation is not on the list, you must apply for a Schengen visa before traveling.

Schengen Visa

If you need a visa, apply for a Schengen visa. The Schengen visa allows you to visit Greece and other Schengen Area countries for up to 90 days during a

180-day period. The application process includes the following steps:

- **Determine the Type of Visa:** Most Ithaca visitors will require a short-stay Schengen visa (Type C) for tourism.
- **Complete the application form**: Fill out the Schengen visa application form, which is normally available on the website of the Greek consulate or embassy in your country.
- **Gather the required documents:** A valid passport, recent passport-sized pictures, a travel itinerary, evidence of accommodation, travel insurance, proof of sufficient finances, and a cover letter describing the purpose of your trip are all commonly necessary documents.
- **Submit the Application:** Submit your application and all necessary documents to the Greek consulate or visa application facility in your country. You might need to arrange an appointment.
- **Pay the Visa Fee:** Pay the non-refundable visa application fee, which is usually around €80 for adults and lower for minors.
- **Attend the Visa Interview:** Certain candidates may be asked to attend a visa interview at the embassy.

- **Wait for Processing:** Visa processing times might vary, so apply well in advance of your scheduled travel dates.

Entry Requirements:

Regardless of whether you need a visa, all travelers must meet the following entry requirements when arriving in Greece:

- **Valid Travel Document:** You must have a passport or national ID card (for EU/EEA citizens) that is valid for at least three months after your intended stay.
- **Proof of accommodation**: If you're staying with friends or family, bring confirmation of your accommodations, such as hotel bookings or a letter from the host.
- **Return or Onward Tickets:** You may be requested to submit proof of a return or onward ticket to show that you intend to depart Greece within the time frame specified.
- **Sufficient funds:** Ensure you have enough money to cover your stay in Greece. This can be shown using bank statements, credit cards, or proof of sponsorship.

- **Travel Insurance:** It is strongly advised to obtain travel insurance that covers medical bills and emergency scenarios during your stay in Greece.

Customs Regulations

Travelers entering Greece should be informed of customs procedures to prevent problems at the crossing. Below are some general guidelines:

- **Prohibited Items:** Certain items are prohibited or restricted from being brought into Greece, such as weapons, narcotics, and protected species. For a fuller list, visit the Greek customs website.
- **Duty-Free Allowances:** EU nationals may import goods for personal use without paying duty. Alcohol, nicotine, and perfumes are all allowed for non-EU passengers. If you exceed these limits, you may have to pay duty.
- **Declaring Items:** If you are carrying large amounts of cash (equivalent to €10,000 or more) or valuable items, you must declare them upon entry.

Ithaca may need some planning and effort, but the trip is well worth it. Whether you arrive by air, boat, or road, you will be met by the island's breathtaking natural beauty and historic heritage. With the proper planning and these travel ideas, you'll be on your way to a fantastic vacation in Ithaca. Have fun on your travels!

Chapter 2
BEST TIME TO VISIT AND DURATION OF STAY

Seasonal Highlights

When planning a trip to Ithaca, knowing the seasonal highlights might make all the difference. I've spent a lot of time on this Greek island, and I can assure you that each season has its own special beauty. Let us break it down:

Spring (March to May)

Springtime in Ithaca is a beautiful time. The island emerges from its winter slumber with a bloom of vibrant wildflowers carpeting the area. The temperatures range from a comfortable 15°C to 25°C (59°F to 77°F), making it ideal for outdoor activities. Hiking routes are especially picturesque this time of year, with lush vegetation and flowering flowers.

A visit to the ancient village of Anogi, perched high on the island, is especially rewarding in spring. The mild weather makes exploring the ancient ruins and the famous Panagia cathedral a pleasurable experience. The community provides spectacular panoramic views of the island's lush mountains and blossoming farms.

Summer (June to August)

Summer is the busiest tourist season in Ithaca, and with good reason. The island's magnificent beaches come alive, and the azure waters are extremely tempting. Temperatures range from 25°C and 35°C (77°F and 95°F), making them perfect for swimming, sunbathing, and water sports.

During the summer, beaches like Filiatro and Gidaki are must-see destinations. Filiatro Beach, with its crystal blue waves and pebbled shoreline, is ideal for families. Gidaki Beach, while more secluded, is a haven for people seeking tranquillity. To get to this jewel, charter a boat from Vathy.

Autumn (September to November)

Autumn is my favourite season in Ithaca. Summer crowds decrease away, but temperatures remain warm and comfortable, ranging from 20°C to 30°C (68°F to 86°F). The sea remains warm enough for swimming, and the island takes on a tranquil, almost magical quality.

This is the ideal moment for cultural immersion. The town of Kion, with its picturesque harbor and quaint tavernas, is especially beautiful in the autumn sunshine. The annual festivals celebrating local harvests and traditional music provide a greater understanding of Ithacan culture.

Winter (December to February)

Winter is the quietest season on the island. Temperatures range between 10°C and 15°C (50°F to 59°F). While it's too chilly to swim, it's an ideal time to discover Ithaca's calm, off-the-beaten-path charm.

Winter is the ideal season to visit the island's cultural and historical treasures without crowds. The Archaeological Site at Alalcomenae and the Cave of the Nymphs are far more accessible. You can also enjoy the friendly ambiance of local cafes and guesthouses, where you can meet locals and learn about daily life in Ithaca.

Ideal Duration for Different Types of Travelers

Weekend Getaway

If you're short on time, a weekend trip to Ithaca can still be extremely rewarding. Concentrate on touring Vathy, the island's capital, and the surrounding attractions. Begin with a visit to the Nautical and Folklore Museum, which provides information on Ithaca's rich nautical heritage.

Spend the afternoons lazing on Filiatro Beach and the nights dining at one of Vathy's many waterfront tavernas. Take a boat journey to Gidaki Beach for a brief adventure.

Cultural Immersion

A week-long stay in Ithaca is great for individuals looking to immerse themselves in the local culture. Begin with the main villages of Vathy, Kioni, and Stavros. Each has its own distinct appeal and historical significance.

Participate in local festivals, which frequently feature traditional music, dance, and cuisine. The Panagia Church in Anogi offers a number of religious festivals that are both spiritual and culturally rich. Visit the local markets to sample fresh produce and handcrafted items.

Outdoor Adventure

Outdoor enthusiasts should budget for at least a week or ten days. Ithaca is ideal for hiking, with numerous trails crisscrossing the island. The trail from Anogi to Kathara Monastery provides breathtaking views and a sense of peace.

Do not miss out on sailing around the island. You can rent a boat in Vathy to explore hidden coves and lesser-known beaches. Snorkeling and diving are also popular activities, with several locations on the island featuring abundant marine life.

Family-friendly trip.

A week is an appropriate length of stay for a family vacation. Ithaca's beaches, such as Filiatro and Dexa, are safe and family-friendly. Spend your days building sand castles and swimming in the calm waters.

Visit the Cave of the Nymphs, a fascinating site for both kids and adults, tied to Homeric legends. The Archaeological Museum of Vathy has interactive exhibits that can keep young ones engaged while teaching them about Ithaca's ancient history.

Budget Travel

Budget travelers can make the most of Ithaca in about five to seven days. Opt for budget-friendly hotels like hostels or family-run guesthouses. Many local tavernas serve wonderful meals at cheap costs.

Exploring the island on foot or by bike is both affordable and rewarding. There are various economical tours that provide a full look at the island's important landmarks without breaking the wallet.

Solo Traveler's Guide

Solo visitors can spend anything from a weekend to a week on Ithaca, depending on their interests. The island is safe and pleasant, with plenty of options for individual exploration.

Spend your days hiking, visiting museums, and relaxing on remote beaches. The local cafés and pubs are fantastic places to meet other visitors and residents, making it easy to make friendships and share experiences.

Romantic Getaways

For couples, a romantic break of four to seven days is great. Spend your days exploring the island's gorgeous scenery and your evenings enjoying romantic dinners at waterfront eateries.

A private boat tour of the island is a necessity. Watch the sunset from the deck as you drink on local wine. The boutique guesthouses in Kioni and Vathy offer charming and cozy accommodations ideal for couples.

In conclusion, Ithaca offers a variety of experiences tailored to different types of travelers. Whether you're visiting for a weekend or planning an extended stay, understanding the best times to visit and the ideal duration for your trip will help you make the most of your time on this enchanting island.

Chapter 3
TOP TOURIST ATTRACTIONS

Vathy: The Charming Capital

Ithaca's capital, Vathy, is a charming and historic town nestled in one of the world's most gorgeous natural bays. Its geographic coordinates are 38.3667° N and 20.7167°E. Vathy serves as the island's heart, combining traditional Greek culture with modern conveniences. The town is known for its Venetian-style architecture, narrow streets, and the serene bay that hugs its coastline.

Exploring Vathy

Waterfront Promenade

Begin your journey in Vathy by strolling down the waterfront promenade. This region is the town's lifeblood, and it is always teeming with activity. The promenade is lined with cafes, taverns, and stores that provide a sense of local life. You may relax here and watch the boats arrive and go while enjoying a cup of Greek coffee and taking in the vibrant environment. The primary promenade area's address is Stratigou Karaiskaki Street.

Archaeological Museum of Ithaca.

The Archaeological Museum of Ithaca, located on Omirou Street in Vathy, 28300, is a must-see attraction. This museum contains a wealth of antiquities from many periods, including the Mycenaean and Roman times. The exhibitions offer an interesting peek into the island's history and the Odysseus legend. Highlights include pottery, tools, and other artifacts discovered at archaeological sites across the island. The museum is well-organized, with thorough explanations in Greek and English.

Panagia Kathariotissa.

The Panagia Kathariotissa, the Cathedral of Ithaca, offers a spiritual and scenic experience. Perched on a hill overlooking Vathy, this cathedral provides panoramic views of the town and the surrounding sea. The address is on a little road rising up from the town center, about one kilometer from the harbor. The interior of the church is embellished with stunning frescoes and icons, and the tranquil atmosphere makes it an ideal location for introspection.

Lazaretto Islet

Lazaretto Islet is located only a short boat trip from Vathy's harbor. This tiny island has a long history, having functioned as a quarantine station and then a jail. Today, it houses the Church of the Savior, which was established in the seventeenth century. The islet is an ideal site for a quick getaway, with a peaceful atmosphere and a touch of history. Boat cruises to Lazaretto depart from the harbor and offer a wonderful opportunity to see this unique landmark.

Maritime and Folklore Museum

The Maritime and Folklore Museum, on Naplionomagniou Street in Vathy, is another cultural jewel. This museum celebrates Ithaca's maritime history and traditional lifestyle. The collection contains ship models, navigation devices, traditional clothing, and historical household objects. It's an excellent site to learn about the island's maritime history and culture.

Dining and Shopping in Vathy

Local Cuisine

Vathy provides a fantastic culinary experience through its numerous tavernas and eateries. Kantouni is one of my personal favorites, located at Mavrokordatou Street, Vathy 28300. This taverna serves traditional Greek cuisine made using fresh, local ingredients. Try the grilled octopus, a local speciality, or the classic moussaka. The welcoming ambiance and view of the port make dining here an unforgettable experience.

For a more upmarket eating experience, visit Libretto Trattoria, located at Loulis Square, Vathy, 28300. This restaurant combines Greek and Italian cuisines, serving delicacies such as shellfish pasta and excellent risotto. The exquisite environment and exceptional service make it ideal for a great evening out.

Shopping

Vathy is also an excellent spot to shop for souvenirs and local products. Kalypso Handmade Jewelry is located at Ethniki Odos Vathiou - Stavrou, Vathy, 28300. Here, you may find stunning handcrafted jewelry inspired by the island's natural beauty and history. Each item is unique, making it an ideal keepsake from your vacation.

Olive Tree Products is another must-see shop, located at Ioanni Metaxa Street, Vathy 28300. This store sells a variety of products derived from local olives, such as olive oil, soap, and cosmetics. The things are of exceptionally high quality and make excellent gifts.

Historic Sites

The House of Odysseus

Don't miss out on seeing the Odysseus House in Vathy. Although the actual site of Odysseus' palace is still debated, local tradition places it near Vathy. The archeological site thought to be related with Odysseus' palace is located in the Pelicata area, near the settlement of Stavros and a short drive from Vathy. The coordinates are 38.4425° North, 20.6625° East. The site provides a fascinating look at ancient Ithaca and its mythical monarch.

Ancient Alalcomenae

Another important historical site near Vathy is the Archaeological Site of Alalcomenae. This archaeological site, located in Piso Aetos, about 3 kilometers from Vathy, has Mycenaean remains. Excavators have discovered the foundations of houses, ceramics, and other artifacts. This site's coordinates are 38.3678°N, 20.6696°E. It's a must-see for history buffs, providing a detailed look into the island's historic past.

Activities and Leisure

Hiking and Nature Walks

Vathy is a good starting point for experiencing the natural splendor of Ithaca. Several hiking paths begin in or pass through the town, providing breathtaking vistas and opportunities to interact with nature. One popular trek leads to the town of Perachori, which is approximately 3 kilometers south of Vathy. The walk winds through olive groves, providing panoramic views of the island

and sea. The trailhead coordinates are 38.3530°N, 20.7160°E.

Boat Rentals and Water Activities

Vathy provides numerous chances for boating and aquatic activities. You can rent a boat at Vathy's harbor and tour the coastline at your leisure. Odyssey Boat Rentals, located at Stratigou Karaiskaki Street, Vathy, 28300, is a dependable rental service. They provide a variety of boats, from little motorboats to larger vessels, ideal for a day out on the water.

Snorkeling and diving are popular pastimes in Vathy. The clean waters surrounding the port are rich with marine life, making it an ideal location for underwater exploration. Local dive companies, such as Ithaca Dive Center in Vathy Harbor, provide guided dives and equipment rentals.

Events & Festivals

Ithaca Cultural Festival

If you visit Vathy in the summer, you may have the opportunity to attend the Ithaca Cultural Festival. This yearly event highlights the island's rich cultural legacy through a variety of performances, exhibitions, and seminars. The festival is normally held in July and August, with events taking place in several sites throughout Vathy, including the main square and the shoreline.

Panagia Kathariotissa Feast.

Another notable festival is the Feast of Panagia Kathariotissa, which takes place on August 15th. This Catholic celebration commemorates the Assumption of the Virgin Mary and features a procession, traditional music, and dance. The Panagia Kathariotissa church serves as the focal point of the celebrations, which pour out onto the town's streets and squares.

Practical Information

Accommodation in Vathy

Vathy offers a range of accommodation options to suit all budgets. The Perantzada Art Hotel, located at Mavrou Gialou Street, Vathy, 28300, is a luxury option. This boutique hotel features contemporary accommodations with breathtaking views of the bay. The hotel's distinctive style and dedicated service make it an excellent choice for discriminating travellers.

For a more affordable choice, visit Hotel Mentor, located at Vathy Harbor, 28300. This hotel has comfortable rooms with balconies overlooking the sea and is conveniently placed near the town's main attractions.

Getting Around

Vathy is a small town, and most of its attractions are within walking distance. However, if you intend to travel further afield, rent a car. Local rental firms, such as Ithaca Rent a Car, located at Vathy Harbor, provide a wide range of vehicles. Bicycles and scooters are also available for rent, providing a fun and convenient mode of transportation.

Kioni: A Picturesque Village

Kioni, located at 38.4167°N, 20.7067°E, is a lovely town on Ithaca's northeastern coast. This enchanting spot is often described as the quintessential Greek village, where time seems to slow down, and every corner is filled with charm and history. Kioni is a spot where you can fully relax and immerse yourself in the island's natural beauty and peacefulness.

Village Overview

Kioni is situated amphitheatrically around a deep blue bay, and its small lanes are lined with historic stone homes, many of which date from the 16th century. The village was mostly spared from the disastrous earthquake that shook the Ionian Islands in 1953, hence its historic architecture is mainly intact. This gives Kioni an authentic and timeless quality that is hard to obtain.

Waterfront and Harbor
Kioni's heart is its harbor, which is located in the village's center. The village's traditional and modern elements are reflected in the colorful fishing boats and magnificent yachts that can be found here. The harbor is surrounded by a row of

cafés and tavernas where you can sit and have a meal or a drink while watching the boats pass by.

Highlights:

- **Margarita Cafe:** Located directly on the shore, this quaint cafe serves delicious coffee and pastries. It's the ideal place to begin your day while admiring the view of the harbor.
- **Taverna Spavento:** Located near the harbor, this taverna is known for its fresh fish and traditional Greek cuisine. Try the grilled octopus or the local dish sofrito.

Historic sites.

Kioni has a rich history, and there are several significant locations to visit while in the area.

Highlights:

- **Church of Agios Nikolaos:** This lovely church, located at the top of the hamlet, is dedicated to Saint Nicholas, the patron saint of sailors. The church has amazing frescoes and provides a tranquil setting for introspection.
- **Old Windmills:** On the outskirts of the village, you'll find the ruins of several old windmills. These windmills, which were previously used to

crush grain, provide a look into the island's agricultural history and an excellent photo opportunity.

Walking and Exploring

Walking is an excellent method to explore Kioni. The village's small, meandering alleyways are ideal for leisurely walks, and you'll find hidden gems around every turn. As you walk, you'll see the vivid bougainvillea spilling down the walls and the aroma of jasmine in the air.

Highlights:

- Kioni Village Trail: This trail starts from the village center and takes you on a scenic walk through olive groves and along the coast. The route provides spectacular views of the harbor and adjacent hills. It's a relatively straightforward trek ideal for people of all ages.
- **Traditional Houses:** As you explore, take note of the traditional stone houses, many of which are adorned with colorful shutters and flower-filled balconies. These houses reflect the village's rich history and craftsmanship.

Beaches Near Kioni

Kioni is surrounded by several beautiful beaches, each offering a unique experience. These beaches are ideal for spending the day relaxing and swimming in the Ionian Sea's crystal-clear waters.

Highlights:

- **Plakoutses Beach:** Just a short walk from the town center, this modest pebble beach is perfect for a brief dip. The water is quite clear, making it ideal for snorkeling.
- **Mavrona Beach:** This private beach, located little further away from the settlement, is ideal for people seeking peace and quiet. The beach is accessible via footpath and surrounded by beautiful greenery.
- **Foki Bay:** About a 10-minute drive from Kioni, Foki Bay is known for its calm, shallow waters and scenic beauty. The beach is family-friendly and has lots of shelter from the nearby olive trees.

Dining in Kioni

Kioni has some fantastic dining options where you may enjoy the flavors of Ionian cuisine. The village's tavernas and eateries take pride in using fresh, local ingredients, particularly seafood.

Highlights:

- **Calypso Restaurant:** Located near the harbor's entrance, Calypso serves traditional Greek cuisine and fresh seafood. The grilled calamari and lamb kleftiko are especially popular.
- **Mythos Taverna:** Located near the harbor, this taverna is noted for its friendly service and delectable cuisine. Don't miss the moussaka or the fresh fish of the day.

Shopping and Souvenirs

Kioni is a small village with a variety of stores selling unique gifts and local items. These businesses are ideal for picking up gifts or souvenirs from your trip.

Highlights:

- **Kioni Boutique:** This charming shop offers a variety of handmade jewelry, ceramics, and textiles. The goods are made by local artists and are excellent mementos.
- **Olive Wood Shop:** This shop specializes in things manufactured from local olive wood, including culinary equipment and ornamental items. Each piece is one-of-a-kind, with superb craftsmanship.

Festivals & Events

If you are fortunate enough to visit Kioni during one of its festivals, you are in for a treat. The hamlet comes alive with music, dancing, and events that showcase the local culture and traditions.

Highlights:

- **Panagias Celebration:** This celebration, held in mid-August, is one of Kioni's most popular festivals. It commemorates the Assumption of the Virgin Mary with a church service, followed by traditional music, dancing, and eating in the village square.
- **Fisherman's Festival:** Celebrated in early summer, this festival honors the village's fishing heritage. The event will feature a boat parade, seafood samples, and live music.

Practical Tips for Visiting Kioni.

Here are a few useful recommendations to help you make the most of your visit to Kioni.

- **Transportation:** Kioni is best explored on foot, although if you're staying further away, renting

a car or scooter is an alternative. There are also regular bus services between Vathy and Kioni.
- **Weather:** The best season to visit Kioni is in the spring and autumn, when the weather is nice and the hamlet is less congested. Summer can be hot, but it's also the busiest season for activities and events.
- **Accommodation:** Kioni offers a range of accommodation options, from traditional guesthouses to modern villas. Booking in advance is recommended, especially during peak season.

Stavros: Heart of Northern Ithaca

Stavros, located at 38.4432° N, 20.6708° E, is a village that truly embodies the spirit of northern Ithaca. Nestled in a lovely valley, it serves as a base for exploring the island's northern regions. Stavros is more than simply a stopover; it's a destination unto itself, full of history, culture, and local charm.

Village Square: The Social Hub.

Stavros' lively village square, located at the intersection of key roads, serves as a convenient meeting location. Locals and visitors alike can enjoy coffee and chat at one of the few traditional cafes. The square is covered by enormous plane trees, which provide a cool retreat even on the hottest days.

The Odysseus monument is one of the village square's highlights. This bronze statue, placed on the southern edge of the square, honors the legendary hero of Homer's epic. It's a popular photo site and a reminder of Ithaca's mythological background.

Archaeological Collection of Stavros

The Archaeological Collection of Stavros, located in the village's center on the main road, is a must-see site. The museum is tiny yet packed with historical objects, including pottery, tools, and jewelry from the Geometric to Roman periods. Among the most intriguing things are those related to the Odyssey, which provide concrete links to the island's mythological past. The museum's address is:

Main Road, Stavros, Ithaca, Greece

Latitude: 38.4432° N, Longitude: 20.6708° E

The Cave of Loizos

Just a short distance from the village is the Cave of Loizos, a significant archaeological and mythological site. The cave is located near the bay of Polis, about 2 kilometers from the center of Stavros. This cave was a place of worship from the Mycenaean period to Roman times, with numerous artifacts discovered here, including offerings to the nymphs and inscriptions dedicated to the gods.

The cave is not easily accessible, and it's best to visit with a local guide who can explain its history and significance. The address for the nearby Polis Bay is:

Polis, Stavros, Ithaca, Greece

Latitude: 38.4500° N, Longitude: 20.6667° E

Polis Beach: A Tranquil Retreat

Polis Beach, situated near the Cave of Loizos, is a tranquil spot perfect for relaxation. The beach is a mix of pebbles and sand, with clear waters ideal for swimming. It's less crowded than some of the more popular beaches on the island, making it a perfect spot for a peaceful day by the sea.

Facilities at Polis Beach are minimal, so it's a good idea to bring your own supplies. The beach is accessible via a short walk from the parking area, which can be found at:

Polis Beach Parking

Polis, Stavros, Ithaca, Greece

Latitude: 38.4500° N, Longitude: 20.6667° E

Pilikata: Archaeological Site

Another must-visit in the Stavros area is the archaeological site of Pilikata, believed to be the location of the ancient city of Ithaca. Excavations here have uncovered remains of houses, walls, and artifacts dating back to the Mycenaean period. The site offers a fascinating glimpse into the island's early history and its connection to the Homeric era.

The site is situated on a hill, offering stunning views of the surrounding area. To visit Pilikata, head to:

Pilikata Archaeological Site

Pilikata, Stavros, Ithaca, Greece

Latitude: 38.4471° N, Longitude: 20.6701° E

Church of the Sotiros

The Church of the Sotiros, located at the edge of Stavros, is another highlight. This church is known for its beautiful frescoes and the annual festival held in honor of the Transfiguration of Christ. The festival, which takes place on August 6th, is a vibrant celebration featuring traditional music, dancing, and local food.

The church itself is a serene place to visit, offering a quiet spot for reflection. The address is:

Church of the Sotiros

Stavros, Ithaca, Greece

Latitude: 38.4452° N, Longitude: 20.6709° E

Local Cuisine and Dining

Stavros offers several excellent dining options where you can sample local cuisine. Taverna Ithaki, located on the main road, is renowned for its traditional Greek dishes, including fresh seafood, souvlaki, and moussaka. The taverna's friendly atmosphere and delicious food make it a favorite among both locals and visitors.

Taverna Ithaki

Main Road, Stavros, Ithaca, Greece

Latitude: 38.4432° N, Longitude: 20.6708° E

For a more casual dining experience, try Rementzo, also located on the main road. This family-run establishment offers a variety of homemade dishes and is particularly known for its hearty breakfasts and friendly service.

Rementzo

Main Road, Stavros, Ithaca, Greece

Latitude: 38.4432° N, Longitude: 20.6708° E

Local Shops and Souvenirs

Stavros is home to several shops where you can purchase local products and souvenirs. Look for handmade jewelry, pottery, and other crafts that reflect the island's rich cultural heritage. One notable shop is Stavros Ceramics, located near the village square, which offers beautifully crafted ceramics inspired by traditional designs.

Stavros Ceramics

Near Village Square, Stavros, Ithaca, Greece

Latitude: 38.4432° N, Longitude: 20.6708° E

Outdoor Activities

For those who enjoy outdoor activities, Stavros is an excellent base for hiking and exploring the natural beauty of northern Ithaca. Several well-marked trails start from the village, leading to scenic viewpoints and historical sites. One popular route is the hike to the Monastery of Kathara, which offers panoramic views of the island and the surrounding sea. The trailhead can be found at:

Monastery of Kathara Trailhead

Stavros, Ithaca, Greece

Latitude: 38.4432° N, Longitude: 20.6708° E

Festivals and Events

Stavros hosts several festivals and events throughout the year that provide a glimpse into local traditions and culture. In addition to the festival at the Church of the Sotiros, there's the Panagia Festival on August 15th, celebrating the Assumption of the Virgin Mary. These festivals are vibrant, community-centered events featuring music, dance, and feasts that are open to all.

Accommodation in Stavros

If you decide to stay in Stavros, there are several accommodation options ranging from budget-friendly guesthouses to more luxurious stays. One highly recommended place is the Stavros Hotel, known for its comfortable rooms and warm hospitality.

Stavros Hotel

Main Road, Stavros, Ithaca, Greece

Latitude: 38.4432° N, Longitude: 20.6708° E

For a more intimate experience, consider staying at a local guesthouse such as Villa Elisa, which offers charming rooms and a peaceful garden setting.

Villa Elisa

Stavros, Ithaca, Greece

Latitude: 38.4432° N, Longitude: 20.6708° E

Practical Tips for Visiting Stavros

- **Getting Around:** Stavros is a compact village, and most attractions are within walking distance. Renting a car or scooter can be useful for exploring the surrounding areas.
- **Local Etiquette:** Stavros is a traditional village, so it's important to respect local customs and dress modestly, especially when visiting churches and religious sites.
- **Best Time to Visit:** The best time to visit Stavros is during the spring and autumn months when the weather is pleasant, and the village is less crowded.

Anogi: Ancient Ruins and Monastery

Anogi, one of Ithaca's oldest and historically significant settlements, is located high in the highlands at an elevation of 500 meters. The village is located at 38.4404°N, 20.6660°E. Anogi feels like stepping back in time, with its unique blend of ancient ruins, traditional Greek culture, and spectacular natural beauty.

Monastery of Panagia Eleousa

The Monastery of Panagia Eleousa is a must-see attraction in Anogi. This monastery, dating back to the 12th century, is an important religious monument on the island. The address is: Monastery of Panagia Eleousa, Anogi, Ithaca, Greece.

Highlights:

- **Historic Frescoes:** The monastery houses some of the island's oldest and most magnificent frescoes. These religious paintings, which show numerous saints and incidents from the Bible, stand out for their brilliant colors and precise detailing.
- **Peaceful atmosphere:** The monastery is a haven of serenity and tranquillity. The only sounds are the occasional ringing of church bells and the calm rustling of the wind through the olive trees.
- **Panoramic Views:** The monastery is set on a hill with extensive views of the island and the Ionian Sea. It's an ideal location for photographers and everyone who likes beautiful scenery.

Menir: The Ancient Standing Stones

Anogi also has a unique collection of ancient standing stones known as the Menir. These massive monoliths are spread around the area and are thought to date back to the Bronze Age. Their purpose is unknown; however local tales say they were employed for religious or ceremonial purposes.

Highlights:

- **Historical Significance:** The Menir are believed to have been placed by the island's ancient inhabitants. They reflect Ithaca's rich and varied history while also adding a sense of mystery to the environment.
- **Scenic walks:** The stones can be found in a variety of locations across the village, making finding them an adventure in itself. Walking amid these ancient monoliths allows you to admire the rough beauty of the Ithaca landscape.
- **Local legends:** According to local legend, the stones possess mystical properties. Some believe they are tied to the island's fabled past and Odysseus mythology. Engaging with these stories can make your trip even more interesting.

The village of Anogi

The village itself is worth exploring. Anogi, with its small alleys, quaint cottages, and friendly residents, provides a look into the true Greek village life. The main village square's address is Anogi Square, Anogi, Ithaca, Greece.

Highlights:

- **Traditional Architecture:** The buildings in Anogi are characteristic of traditional Ionian architecture. Many cottages have survived for generations, with stone walls and terracotta roofs that add to the village's attractiveness.
- **Local Tavernas:** There are a few tiny tavernas in the area that serve traditional Greek cuisine. Locally sourced ingredients such as olive oil, fresh veggies, and seafood make for delectable dishes.
- **Church of the Dormition:** Located in the heart of the village, this church is another significant religious site. It has a lovely bell tower and is a hub for local activity, particularly during religious festivals.

Practical information

- **Getting There:** Anogi can be reached by automobile or taxi from Vathy, the island's capital. The ride takes roughly 30 minutes and includes stunning sights along the route. There are few public transit choices, so hiring a car is essential if you want to see more of the island.
- **Best Time to Visit:** The best time to visit Anogi is during the spring and autumn months when the weather is mild and the landscape is lush and green. Summer can be scorching, but it also brings the town to life with a variety of festivals and events.

Tips for Travelers:

- Footwear: Wear comfortable shoes designed for walking on uneven terrain, especially if you intend to explore the Menir.
- **Water and Snacks:** Bring water and snacks because there are few places to get refreshments in the village.
- **Respect Local Customs:** Remember that the monastery and churches are places of worship. Dress modestly and respect the local customs and traditions.

Filiatro Beach: A Beach Paradise

Filiatro Beach is a hidden gem on Ithaca's eastern shore, only a few kilometers from the island's capital, Vathy. The exact coordinates are 38.3560° N, 20.7260° E, and the beach is readily reached by automobile or a short boat journey from Vathy. This beach is notable for its crystal-clear seas, silky white pebbles, and lush green surroundings of olive groves and pine trees, which make a tranquil and scenic environment.

Getting to Filiatro Beach

Filiatro Beach is around a 10-minute drive from Vathy. Travel southeast on Andrea Tsatsou and follow the signs to Filiatro. The road is paved and in good shape, making for an easy ride. If you prefer, you can take a taxi from Vathy; the ride is quick and usually inexpensive.

Boats are available for lease at Vathy harbor for people seeking excitement. Renting a small boat allows you to explore Filiatro Beach at your own leisure and visit other surrounding coves and beaches.

Beach Amenities and Facilities

Filiatro Beach is well-organized and provides a variety of amenities to ensure a pleasant visit. Here's a rundown of what you should expect:

- **Sunbeds and Umbrellas:** Available for rent, providing comfort and shade for a relaxing day by the sea. The cost is usually modest, between €5 and €10 per day.
- **Beach Bar:** A small bar on the beach serves a selection of drinks, snacks, and light meals. It's the ideal place to sip a crisp cocktail or a cold beer while admiring the vista.
- **Restrooms and Showers:** Facilities are available, making it convenient for families and those planning to spend the entire day at the beach.
- **Parking**: Free parking is available near the beach. However, it might fill up rapidly during peak season, so it's best to come early.

Activities at Filiatro Beach

Filiatro Beach offers a variety of activities that cater to varied interests, not only lazing in the sun.

- **Swimming**: Filiatro Beach's quiet, clean waters are great for swimming. The moderate slope of the seabed makes it suitable for swimmers of all abilities, especially children.
- **Snorkeling**: Bring your snorkeling gear and discover the aquatic world. The visibility is good, and you can observe a wide range of marine life, including colorful fish and sea urchins.
- **Kayaking and Paddleboarding**: Rentals are available at the beach bar. Paddling along the shore is an excellent opportunity to enjoy the beautiful views and discover adjacent coves.
- **Beach Volleyball:** There is a specific space for beach volleyball, which is ideal for those seeking friendly competition.

Best time to visit

The greatest time to visit Filiatro Beach is between June and September, when the weather is warm and sunny. The sea temperature ranges from 22°C (72°F) in June to 26°C (79°F) in August, making it ideal for swimming.

If you prefer a more tranquil experience, go in the early morning or late afternoon. The beach is less crowded during these hours, allowing you to experience the peace and beauty of Filiatro without the congestion and bustle of the midday sun.

Nearby Attractions

Filiatro Beach's position makes it the ideal starting point for exploring other surrounding sites.

- **Gidaki Beach:** Another beautiful beach accessible by boat or hiking trail from Filiatro. Gidaki Beach is famous for its remoteness and clear waves. Coordinates: 38.3667° North, 20.7167° East.
- **Skino Bay:** Located just north of Filiatro, Skino Bay offers a more rugged and natural beach experience. It's ideal for anyone who prefer visiting off-the-beaten-path destinations.
- **Perachori Village:** A lovely village located inland of Filiatro. It's worth going to experience traditional Ithacan living and eat local cuisine at one of the village tavernas.

Practical tips for visiting Filiatro Beach

- **Bring Cash:** While the beach bar and several amenities take credit cards, it's best to have cash for rentals and small purchases.
- **Sun Protection:** The Mediterranean sun can be harsh, so carry sunscreen, hats, and sunglasses to shield yourself from UV radiation.

- **Water and Snacks:** While there is a beach bar, carrying your own water and snacks can be beneficial, especially if you have dietary restrictions.
- **Early arrival:** To guarantee a decent spot and escape the crowds, arrive early in the morning.

Address for Navigation.

If you're using a GPS or a map application to travel to Filiatro Beach, use the following address:

Filiatro beach, Ithaca 283 00, Greece

Gidaki Beach: Secluded Beauty

Gidaki Beach, located at 38.3667° N, 20.7167° E, is one of Ithaca's most beautiful and secluded beaches. This hidden gem provides a tranquil and pure atmosphere, ideal for anyone seeking to avoid the crowds and experience nature at its best. Gidaki, unlike many other beaches on the island, is only accessible by boat or foot, adding to its pristine charm and tranquility.

Getting to Gidaki Beach

There are two primary ways to reach Gidaki Beach: by boat or by hiking.

By boat

The most convenient method to get to Gidaki Beach is by boat. During the tourist season, regular boat tours sail from Vathy's harbor (latitude 38.3667° N, longitude 20.7167° E). These tours normally last 15-20 minutes and provide spectacular views of Ithaca's coastline. You can schedule a ride with local operators like Captain Nikos or Odysseus Cruises, who offer dependable and pleasurable service. Prices are typically affordable, and some operators provide round-trip tickets with variable return schedules, allowing you to spend as much time as you want on the beach.

By hiking

For the more adventurous, a hike to Gidaki Beach is a rewarding experience. The walk begins near the southern end of Vathy, specifically at Dexa Beach (38.3578° N, 20.7211° E). The hike lasts around 45 minutes to an hour, depending on your speed and physical level. The path is well-marked, but it can be steep and rocky in sections, so strong shoes are required. Along the trip, you'll enjoy panoramic views of the Ionian Sea and Ithaca's rich flora. It is best to start early in the morning to avoid the midday heat, and bring lots of water and food.

Beach Highlights:

Gidaki Beach is well-known for its crystal-clear blue seas and fine white stones, which create a picture-perfect environment. The following are some of the highlights you can enjoy during your visit:

Swimming and Snorkeling

Gidaki Beach's waters are extremely clear, making it suitable for swimming and snorkeling. The calm waves and steady depth increase make it suitable for swimmers of all abilities. If you bring snorkeling equipment, you'll be able to explore the underwater environment, which is home to a diverse range of marine life, including colorful fish and beautiful rock formations.

Seclusion and serenity

Gidaki Beach's remoteness is one of its most appealing aspects. Unlike more accessible beaches, Gidaki is usually peaceful and empty, even during peak tourist season. This makes it a wonderful place to relax and unwind. You can choose a tranquil location to lay down your towel and listen to the waves without the normal throng and bustle.

Natural beauty

The natural beauty of Gidaki Beach is really amazing. Surrounded by steep cliffs and lush foliage, the beach provides a sense of solitude and connection to nature. The contrast between the white pebbles, turquoise waves, and green backdrop produces a breathtaking visual feast. It's an ideal spot for photographers seeking to capture the essence of Ithaca's pristine landscapes.

Practical information

What to bring

Given its isolated location, Gidaki Beach lacks amenities. Therefore, it is vital to come prepared. Here's a checklist of what you should bring:

- **Sun protection:** hat, sunglasses, and sunscreen.
- **Food and Drinks:** There are no kiosks or restaurants, so bring a picnic with lots of water, snacks, and lunch.
- **Comfort:** Beach towel, blanket, or portable chair
- **Snorkeling Gear:** If you wish to explore the underwater scenery, bring a mask, snorkel, and fins.
- **Waste Bags:** Remember to take all of your rubbish with you to help keep the beach clean.

Safety Tips

- **Footwear**: The hike to the beach can be challenging, so wear sturdy shoes with good grip.
- **Water Safety:** The seas are normally calm, but be aware of changing conditions and avoid swimming too far from the beach.
- **Sun Protection:** Because there is little natural shade, you should wear sunscreen, especially during the hottest parts of the day.

Nearby Attractions

While Gidaki Beach is a must-see, there are other local sights worth exploring:

Dexa Beach

If you opt to hike to Gidaki, you'll start at Dexa Beach (38.3578° N, 20.7211° E). Dexa is a magnificent place in its own right, with tranquil waters and a relaxing environment. It's an ideal location to unwind before or after your hike. Legend has it that this is where Odysseus landed on his return to Ithaca, bringing a bit of mythological mystery to your visit.

Skinos Beach

Skinos Beach, located at 38.3610° N and 20.7350° E, is another local beach worth visiting. Skinos, located east of Gidaki, is famed for its shallow seas and peaceful atmosphere. It's ideal for families and anyone seeking a quieter beach experience. Skinos is accessible via a coastal trail from Vathy that provides stunning views along the way.

The Archaeological Site of Alalcomenae: Historical Insights

The Archaeological Site of Alalcomenae, located near the quiet village of Piso Aetos at 38.3678° N, 20.6696° E, is one of Ithaca's most intriguing historical sites. This antiquity-rich location provides a profound view into the ancient world, particularly the Mycenaean civilization that formerly thrived here.

Historical significance

The site of Alalcomenae is said to be linked to the legendary city of Alalcomenae, which is referenced in several ancient sources. Excavators have discovered major artifacts and constructions from the Mycenaean period (about 1600-1100 BC). This was a time when Ithaca was a thriving center of activity, inextricably linked to the larger Mycenaean culture that dominated most of Greece.

What to Expect

Ancient Foundations and Structures

When you arrive at the site, which is just off the main road connecting Vathy and Stavros, you'll observe the foundations of what were once majestic buildings. The layout of these structures implies a well-organized settlement, with separate areas for dwelling, working, and socializing. Walking among these ruins, it's easy to imagine the thriving community that once inhabited this ancient town.

Artifacts and Pottery

The enormous collection of pottery shards and other items discovered at Alalcomenae is one of the site's most notable features. These items are frequently intricately decorated, revealing details about the ancient Ithacans' artistic abilities and daily lives. Some of the more notable artifacts, such as ceremonial pots and implements, are on exhibit at the Vathy Archaeological Museum, providing a more complete understanding of their use and significance.

Tholos Tomb

The Tholos Tomb, a massive, beehive-shaped burial building typical of Mycenaean construction, is one of the site's most famous features. These tombs were used to bury prominent figures, and the one at Alalcomenae is no exception. The tomb's enormous stones and complex design demonstrate the Mycenaeans' engineering prowess and reverence for the deceased.

Terraced fields

Terraced fields utilized for agriculture can be found all around the main settlement. These terraces are a clever adaption to Ithaca's mountainous environment, allowing the ancient inhabitants to successfully farm crops. Exploring these fields gives you a feeling of the creativity and resourcefulness that defined Mycenaean society.

Practical Information

Address and Access

The property is easily accessible via the main road that connects Vathy to Stavros. If coming from Vathy, drive for around 20 minutes northwest on the EO Vathiou-Stavrou route. Look for signs leading you to Piso Aetos, and you'll see it well marked along the road.

Visitor Tips:

- **Wear Comfortable Shoes:** Since the terrain might be uneven, solid footwear is recommended.
- **Bring Water and Snacks:** There are no amenities on-site, so bring your own refreshments.
- **Best time to visit:** Early morning or late afternoon visits are great for escaping the midday heat and enjoying the site in a more tranquil atmosphere.

Nearby Attractions

While you're in the region, there are a few additional attractions to check out in addition to Alalcomenae.

Piso Aetos Beach.

Piso Aetos Beach (38.3617° N, 20.6617° E) is only a short drive from the archeological site and provides a peaceful place to unwind after exploration. The clean waters provide for a delightful swim, while the pebbled shore is ideal for sunbathing.

Monastery of Panagia Eleousa

This monastery, located a few kilometers distant in the village of Anogi (38.4404° N, 20.6660° E), is another historical gem. The journey to the monastery takes you via gorgeous paths, and the monastery itself is a peaceful place with stunning frescoes and panoramic views of the island.

Highlights

- **Connection to Homeric Legends**

The site's association with the Homeric epics heightens its mystery. Alalcomenae is frequently associated with the stories of Odysseus, Ithaca's legendary monarch. As you wander among the remains, contemplate the potential that Homeric heroes were familiar with this very location.

- **Educational Tours**

If you want to go deeper into history, try arranging a guided tour. Knowledgeable guides can share fascinating stories and insights that bring the ancient ruins to life. These tours are frequently offered from local tour operators in Vathy or Stavros.

- **Photography Opportunities**

The site offers numerous opportunities for photography enthusiasts. The juxtaposition between the ancient ruins and Ithaca's natural beauty creates a magnificent backdrop for creating unique photos.

Aetos: Ancient Ruins and Modern Views

Aetos (Greek for "eagle") is between the villages of Vathy and Piso Aetos and is a historical and archaeological treasure trove. This location, located at 38.3667° N, 20.6767° E, is recognized for its important Mycenaean remains and boasts some of the most spectacular vistas on the island. Aetos is a must-see attraction for those who want to learn more about Ithaca's rich history.

Mycenaean Settlement

Aetos is home to one of the most significant Mycenaean archeological sites in the Ionian Islands. The ancient acropolis, known as the "Castle of Aetos," dates back to the 2nd millennium BCE. The property is situated on the ridge between the bays of Vathy and Piso Aetos, offering strategic views of the surrounding area.

Highlights of the Mycenaean Site

The Acropolis

The acropolis rises atop the hill, providing panoramic views of the island and the sea. Walking around the ruins, you can observe the remnants of ancient walls and foundations that were once part of a fortified settlement.

Address: Aetos Ridge, Ithaca, Greece (No formal address; follow signs from Vathy or Piso Aetos).

Cyclopean walls

These large limestone slabs, typical of Mycenaean architecture, are called after the mythical Cyclops due to their immense size. The walls formed part of the fortifications that guarded the acropolis against intruders.

Highlight: The craftsmanship and engineering of these walls are exceptional, demonstrating the superior talents of Mycenaean builders.

Tholos Tomb

This beehive-shaped tomb, found near the acropolis, is one of Aetos' most notable discovery. Tholos tombs were primarily reserved for high-ranking persons, demonstrating the settlement's prominence.

Highlight: The tomb's construction and the artifacts found within provide valuable insights into Mycenaean burial practices and social hierarchy.

Modern Views

While the ancient remains of Aetos provide an insight into Ithaca's rich history, the area itself offers some of the best modern vistas on the island. The acropolis ridge's elevated position provides extensive views of Ithaca's natural splendor and the surrounding waterways.

Highlights of the Views
Bay of Vathy

From the acropolis, you can see the tranquil waters of Vathy Bay, which has a sheltered port and the town of Vathy stretched out along the coast. The vista is especially breathtaking around sunset, when the sky transforms into a magnificent display of colors.

Photo Opportunity: This vantage point is ideal for capturing panoramic views of the bay and town.

Piso Aetos Bay.

Piso Aetos Bay, located to the west, has similarly stunning vistas. This quieter side of the island offers a rockier and natural landscape, with fewer houses and more pristine beaches.

Highlight: The contrast between the peaceful sea and the towering hills is stunning, making it an ideal location for landscape photography.

Surrounding Countryside

The hills and valleys surrounding Aetos are covered with olive groves, cypress trees, and traditional stone cottages. The lush foliage and old structures enhance the picturesque appeal of the area.

Tip: Bring binoculars to fully appreciate the details of the landscape and perhaps spot some local wildlife.

Practical information

Getting to Aetos.

Aetos is accessible by car or foot. If you are driving from Vathy, take the main road to Piso Aetos. The trek is around 6 kilometers long and takes about 15 minutes. For those who prefer trekking, there are various pathways leading up to the Acropolis, some of which are fairly steep and demand a moderate level of fitness.

- **By Car:** From Vathy, follow the signs to Piso Aetos. There is limited parking near the site, so arrive early to reserve your spot.
- **On Foot:** Hiking paths begin in Vathy and Piso Aetos. The trail from Vathy is more difficult, but the one from Piso Aetos is shorter and easier.

What to Bring

- **Comfortable Footwear:** The terrain can be uneven and rocky, so strong footwear is required.
- **Water and Snacks:** There are no amenities on site, so bring your own refreshments.
- **Sun Protection:** The region is exposed and has little shade. Hats, sunscreen, and sunglasses are all suggested.
- **Camera**: The views are breathtaking, and you'll want to photograph them.

Nearby Attractions

While exploring Aetos, consider visiting some nearby sites to enhance your experience.

Piso Aetos Port

This little harbor serves as a gateway to Ithaca, with boats linking the island with the mainland. It's a peaceful location with a few cafes where you can unwind and enjoy the sea views.

Address: Piso Aetos, Ithaca, Greece

Anogi Village

Anogi, located just a short drive from Aetos, is one of Ithaca's oldest villages. It is famous for the Monastery of Panagia Eleousa and the enigmatic Menir standing stones.

Highlight: The panoramic views from Anogi match those of Aetos, while the settlement itself is rich in history.

Stavros Village

Another nearby village, Stavros, has a lovely square, local shops, and the Archaeological Collection of Stavros. It's an excellent place to experience local life and visit extra historical places.

Highlight: The Cave of Loizos, located just outside Stavros, adds another dimension of myth and history to your journey.

Lazaretto Islet: Historical Landmark

Lazaretto Islet, also known as the Island of the Saviors, is a small island in the bay of Vathy, the capital of Ithaca. Its geographic coordinates are roughly 38.3625° N latitude and 20.7140° E longitude. Despite its tiny size, Lazaretto Islet is an important part of Ithaca's history and provides tourists with a unique perspective on the island's past.

Historical significance

Lazaretto Islet has a rich and diverse history. During the Venetian time, the island served as a quarantine facility to prevent the spread of infectious diseases. Ships arriving in Ithaca were compelled to dock at the islet, where passengers and crew were quarantined if they were suspected of being ill. This method helped to safeguard the island's people from diseases, which were prevalent at the time.

Later, in the 19th century, the islet had a new role. It was converted as a prison, primarily for political inmates. The remains of these facilities are still evident today, serving as a stark reminder of the islet's past.

Highlights of Lazaretto Islet

Church of the Savior

The Church of the Savior is a significant attraction on Lazaretto Islet. This lovely chapel, built in the 17th century, is the only edifice left from the island's period as a quarantine facility. The church was rebuilt in the twentieth century and remains a tranquil and lovely site of worship.

Address: Lazaretto Islet, Bay of Vathy, Ithaca, Greece

Highlights: The church's basic but attractive architecture, serene ambiance, and breathtaking views of Vathy from the islet make it a must-see.

Visiting the Islet

Visiting Lazaretto Islet is a wonderful experience. Small boats routinely depart from Vathy's harbor, providing a quick and scenic voyage to the islet. The drive itself is enjoyable, since you can see panoramic views of Vathy and the surrounding region.

- **Boat Departure Point:** Vathy Harbor, Ithaca, Greece (38.3667° N, 20.7167° E)
- **Boat Ride Duration:** Approximately 10 minutes
- **Cost**: Varies by boat operator; typically around €5-€10 per person

Exploring the Islet

Upon arriving, you will see a walkway leading to the Church of the Savior. The stroll is easy and only takes a few minutes. The island is small enough to explore extensively in a short period of time, but it's also the ideal place to relax, snap photos, and soak in the peaceful atmosphere.

Highlights: Panoramic views of Vathy, the historical ruins of the quarantine and prison facilities, and the peaceful setting of the Church of the Savior.

Tips: Wear comfortable shoes because the terrain can be uneven. Bring water and a hat for sun protection, especially in the summer.

Practical Information

Accessibility

Lazaretto Islet is only accessible by boat. The short voyage from Vathy is normally smooth, but you should always check the weather and sea conditions before organizing your trip. Although the islet is generally straightforward to explore, tourists with mobility limitations may find the rough ground unsuitable.

Best time to visit

The best time to visit Lazaretto Islet is in the spring and summer (April to October), when the weather is nice and the sea is quiet. The island is accessible year-round, but boat services may be limited during the winter months.

Visiting Ithaca's top tourist attractions provides an ideal blend of history, culture, and natural beauty. Each place has a unique tale to tell, and when combined, they provide a rich and immersive experience. Whether you're visiting ancient ruins, relaxing on pristine beaches, or meandering through charming villages, Ithaca never fails to enchant and inspire.

Chapter 4

ITINERARIES FOR DIFFERENT TRAVELERS

Weekend Getaway

Day 1: Arrival and Initial Exploration

Morning:

- Arrive early in Vathy, the charming capital of Ithaca.
- Check into your accommodation.
- Stroll along the waterfront and enjoy a coffee at a local cafe.

Afternoon:

- Have lunch at Kantouni, a traditional taverna offering delicious Greek dishes.
- Visit the Archaeological Museum of Vathy to learn about the island's rich history.

Evening:

- Head to Filiatro Beach, one of the closest beaches to Vathy, for a swim and sunset views.

- Dine at Rementzo, a restaurant known for its fantastic views and local cuisine.

Day 2: Adventure and Relaxation

Morning:

- Visit the Cave of the Nymphs, a site steeped in mythology.
- Wear comfortable shoes for the hike to the cave.

Afternoon:

- Drive to the picturesque village of Kioni for lunch at Taverna Avra.
- Spend the afternoon at Gidaki Beach, known for its stunning beauty and clear waters.

Evening:

- Return to Vathy for some nightlife.
- Enjoy cocktails and live music at Beba's.

Cultural Immersion

Day 1: Historical Insights

Morning:

- Begin at the Archaeological Museum of Vathy.
- Learn about the island's extensive history through the artifacts.

Afternoon:

- Visit the Kathara Monastery for both spiritual insight and breathtaking views.
- Have lunch at Taverna Poseidon in Vathy, known for its authentic Greek dishes.
- Explore the village of Anogi, home to the Anogi Monastery and ancient ruins.

Evening:

- Return to Vathy and enjoy a leisurely evening stroll or a quiet dinner at a local taverna.

Day 2: Local Traditions and Cuisine

Morning:

- Visit the Vathy Market to interact with locals and buy fresh produce.
- Engage with vendors to learn about Ithacan traditions and daily life.

Afternoon:

- Participate in a cooking class in Stavros, learning to make traditional Greek dishes like spanakopita and baklava.
- End your day with a visit to the Tsantali Vineyards for a tour and tasting session.

Evening:

- Enjoy a peaceful evening with a homemade meal or dine out at a cozy local restaurant.

Outdoor Adventure

Day 1: Hiking and Scenic Views

Morning:

- Start with a hike to the peak of Mount Neriton for breathtaking views of the island.
- Pack a picnic to enjoy at the summit.

Afternoon:

- Descend and visit the village of Exogi, known for its stunning landscapes and additional hiking trails.
- Enjoy lunch at a local taverna in Exogi.

Evening:

- Return to your accommodation and relax after a day of hiking.
- Opt for a quiet dinner or explore a local bar.

Day 2: Water Adventures

Morning:

- Rent a kayak in Vathy and explore the coastline.
- Discover hidden coves and secluded beaches.

Afternoon:

- Pack a lunch to enjoy on a quiet beach.
- Continue exploring the waters around Ithaca.

Evening:

- Return to Vathy and enjoy a relaxing evening.
- Have dinner at a waterfront restaurant and reflect on the day's adventures.

Family-Friendly Trip

Day 1: Interactive Exploration

Morning:

- Start at the Archaeological Museum of Vathy, which has exhibits engaging for all ages.
- Let the kids explore and learn about the island's history.

Afternoon:

- Visit the charming village of Kioni for lunch and let the kids play by the sea.
- Spend the afternoon at Filiatro Beach, which is family-friendly with shallow waters and facilities.

Evening:

- Return to Vathy for a family dinner.
- Enjoy an evening walk or visit a local park.

Day 2: Fun and Learning

Morning:

- Take a guided tour to the Cave of the Nymphs, where mythology comes to life.
- Engage the kids with stories of Odysseus and the nymphs.

Afternoon:

- Head to Stavros for a family cooking class.
- Learn to make traditional Greek dishes together.

Evening:

- Spend the evening at a local park or play area in Vathy.
- Enjoy a casual dinner at a family-friendly restaurant.

Budget Travel

Day 1: Economical Exploration

Morning:

- Walk around Vathy, visiting free attractions like the harbor and public parks.
- Take in the sights and sounds of the town.

Afternoon:

- Have an affordable meal at a local taverna.
- Spend the afternoon at a free-entry beach like Sarakiniko.

Evening:

- Explore local markets and enjoy street food for dinner.
- Relax at your accommodation or visit a local bar for a budget-friendly evening.

Day 2: Affordable Adventures

Morning:

- Take a budget-friendly hike to Mount Neriton.
- Pack a picnic to enjoy along the way.

Afternoon:

- Continue exploring the hiking trails around Exogi.
- Visit local villages and interact with the residents.

Evening:

- Enjoy dinner at a local taverna known for its affordable and delicious meals.
- Spend a quiet evening enjoying the local culture.

Solo Traveler's Guide

Day 1: Solo Exploration

Morning:

- Enjoy the freedom to explore Vathy at your own pace.

- Visit the Archaeological Museum and wander the streets of the town.

Afternoon:

- Have lunch at a cozy cafe, people-watching and soaking in the atmosphere.
- Spend the afternoon at a tranquil beach like Gidaki.

Evening:

- Find a lively bar like Beba's to meet fellow travelers.
- Enjoy a solo dinner at a waterfront restaurant.

Day 2: Personal Adventure

Morning:

- Take a solo hike to Mount Neriton or explore the trails around Exogi.
- Engage with locals at a market or join a group tour for social interaction.

Afternoon:

- Continue your personal adventure, discovering hidden spots and scenic views.
- Relax at a quiet beach or visit another village.

Evening:

- Enjoy dinner at a local taverna.
- Reflect on your solo journey and plan for the next day's adventures.

Romantic Getaways

Day 1: Romantic Scenery

Morning:

- Begin with a romantic breakfast at a waterfront cafe in Vathy.
- Visit the picturesque village of Kioni for lunch and a peaceful stroll.

Afternoon:

- Spend the afternoon at a secluded beach like Gidaki, perfect for couples.
- Enjoy a swim and relax by the clear waters.

Evening:

- Have a romantic dinner at Rementzo, overlooking the harbor as the sun sets.
- Take a moonlit walk along the waterfront.

Day 2: Love and Adventure

Morning:

- Hike together to the Cave of the Nymphs.
- Share stories and enjoy the beautiful scenery.

Afternoon:

- Visit the Tsantali Vineyards for a wine tasting and tour.
- Have lunch at a scenic spot, enjoying each other's company.

Evening:

- Enjoy a quiet evening at your accommodation or explore a local bar.
- Reflect on your romantic getaway and plan for future travels together.

These itineraries provide a variety of options tailored to different interests and travel styles, ensuring a memorable and fulfilling visit to Ithaca, Greece. Whether you're on a weekend getaway, seeking cultural immersion, or embarking on an outdoor adventure, Ithaca offers something special for every traveler.

Chapter 5

PRACTICAL TIPS

Health and Safety Precautions

Ithaca visitors must prioritize their health and safety. Let me offer some vital tips I've learned during my trips.

First and foremost, always keep a basic first-aid kit with you. Although Ithaca is generally safe and well-equipped, it is always prudent to be prepared for minor accidents or illnesses. Pharmacies are available in Vathy, the island's capital, but having bandages, antiseptic wipes, and pain medicines on hand can save you a trip.

Staying hydrated is critical, especially in the hot months. The Greek sun may be very hot, and dehydration can sneak up on you. Always carry a water bottle, and if possible, use reusable ones to help reduce plastic waste. Tap water is fine to drink, although you may prefer bottled water, which is widely accessible.

Concerning food safety, I've never had a problem eating at local tavernas or street sellers. The meal is fresh, flavorful, and carefully prepared. If you have a delicate stomach, start with familiar dishes before experimenting with more experimental local cuisine.

The nearest major medical center for health crises is the General Hospital of Cephalonia, which is located on the nearby island of Cephalonia. On Ithaca, there is a smaller health center in Vathy. The team is professional and capable of handling most medical issues. Always keep a copy of your health insurance and emergency contact information with you.

Communication and Language Tips

Interacting with locals is one of the most enjoyable aspects of travel. While many people in Ithaca speak English, particularly in tourist areas, knowing a few Greek phrases will help you enjoy your visit. The locals appreciate it when you make an attempt to speak their language, even if it's as basic as saying "Kalimera" (Good morning) or "Efharisto" (Thank you).

Greek can be difficult, so don't stress about perfect pronunciation. I've found that a smile and genuine effort go a long way. Here are some handy phrases.

- "Parakaló" (Please)
- "Signomi" (Excuse me/Sorry)
- "Pou ine i toualéta?" (Where is the bathroom?)
- "Poso kostízei?" (How much does it cost?)
- "To logariasmó parakaló" (The bill, please)

You can also download a translation app or carry a small phrasebook. Most signs in Ithaca are bilingual, so navigating should be relatively straightforward.

Local Etiquette and Customs

Understanding and respecting local customs is essential for a great travel experience. In Ithaca, the pace of life is slower, and people value politeness and hospitality. Here are some etiquette points to bear in mind:

- **Greetings:** When meeting someone for the first time, a handshake is expected. Friends typically kiss on both cheeks. Saying "Kalimera" (Good morning), "Kalispera" (Good evening), or "Yassou" (Hello) is a kind gesture.
- **Dress Code:** While Ithaca is casual, modest clothes is preferred, especially when visiting

churches or religious places. Beachwear is appropriate on the beach, but not in town.
- **Dining:** Mealtimes in Greece are social occasions. Lunch is typically served between 1-3 PM, while dinner frequently begins around 8 PM. It is traditional to share dishes, so do not be shocked if your host orders multiple plates for the table. If you're welcomed to someone's home, bringing a small gift, such as flowers or cookies, is a good gesture.
- **Respect for Sites:** Ithaca is steeped in history and mythology. When visiting archaeological sites or monuments, adhere to the rules and respect the environment. Photography is generally permitted, but please check for any limitations.
- **Tipping**: While not required, it is appreciated. In restaurants, it is usual to leave approximately 10% of the bill. Taxis frequently round up their fares.

By following these suggestions, you'll fit in smoothly and experience the wonderful friendliness that Ithacans are known for.

Chapter 6

TRANSPORTATION WITHIN ITHACA

Public Transport Options

When I landed in Ithaca, one of my first duties was to figure out how to get around the island efficiently. The public transport system, though limited compared to larger cities, is quite practical for getting around Ithaca.

The mainstay of public transportation here is the bus service, operated by the local bus company. The majority of the island's significant destinations, including the capital, Vathy, and popular villages such as Kioni and Stavros, are accessible by bus. Vathy's bus station is centrally positioned, making it easy to discover and access. I recommend checking the bus schedules at the station or online, as they sometimes change, especially during the off-peak season. Fares are normally between €2 and €5, depending on distance, and tickets can be purchased straight from the driver.

Traveling by bus not only saves money, but also gives a scenic trip across the island's beautiful scenery. The travel between settlements is a pleasure in itself, with sights of verdant countryside, olive trees, and breathtaking coastal views. While buses are often prompt, it is always a good idea to leave some extra time in your itinerary, especially if you have connecting activities.

Taxis offer more immediate or personalized transportation. Taxi stands are available in Vathy and other main areas, or you can call one. Fares can be negotiated, particularly for longer excursions or tours. A regular fare from Vathy to Kioni may cost between €20 and €30. It's useful to have the phone numbers of a few taxi drivers; many locals rely on taxis for their dependability and convenience, especially when going with luggage or after hours.

Car Rental and Driving Tips

Renting a car in Ithaca provides you the flexibility to explore at your own speed. Vathy has various rental agencies, as do several of the larger towns, such as Frikes. I found it advantageous to reserve a car ahead of time, especially during the peak season from June to September.

Driving in Ithaca is generally a pleasant experience; nevertheless, there are a few items to be aware of:

- **Road Conditions:** The main roads are in good condition, but expect narrow, winding roads in the more rural sections. These can be very steep and winding, so drive carefully.
- **Traffic:** Traffic is light compared to urban areas, but during summer, the roads can become busier with tourists. Always be prepared for slower-moving vehicles and the rare livestock crossing.
- **Parking:** Parking can be challenging in the smaller villages. Look for appropriate parking spaces and avoid obstructing tiny streets or local entry points.
- **Fuel:** There are a few petrol stations on the island, mostly in Vathy. It is advisable to fill up before embarking on longer drives.

Having a car allows you to visit some of the more remote beaches, such as Aspros Gialos or Gidaki, and have the option to stop whenever a view catches your eye.

Biking and Walking Routes

Biking and walking are fantastic methods for more adventurous and environmentally conscientious travelers to discover Ithaca. The island's modest size makes it excellent for cycling and hiking.

- **Biking:** There are several bicycle rental shops in Vathy and Kioni. Mountain bikes are recommended because of the hilly terrain. Popular bike routes include the picturesque coastline road from Vathy to Kioni and the route from Stavros to Anogi hamlet, which provide stunning views of the island's rough terrain.
- **Walking:** Ithaca is a walker's heaven. Well-marked trails traverse the island, taking you through forests, along cliffs, and past ancient ruins. Some of my favorite walks are:
- **Vathy to Perachori:** This moderate climb takes you from the harbor town of Vathy to the traditional village of Perachori, with breathtaking views of the bay.
- **Anogi to Exogi:** This trail leads through lovely mountain communities, providing panoramic

views and opportunities to visit the island's famous monoliths.
- **Frikes to Kioni:** A seaside trail winding through olive orchards and along cliffs, ideal for a relaxing afternoon stroll.

Boat Rentals and Water Taxi

Given Ithaca's maritime past, boat tours are a must. Several enterprises in Vathy, Kioni, and Frikes rent boats, ranging from tiny motorboats to larger yachts. Renting a boat allows you to visit hidden beaches and coves that are otherwise inaccessible.

- **Boat Rentals:** Small motorboats can be rented without a license and are suitable for day trips along the coast. Prices normally start between €70 and €100 per day, plus fuel. Larger boats and yachts can be chartered with a skipper to provide a more luxurious experience.
- **Water Taxis:** For quick trips between coastal settlements or visits to surrounding islets, water taxis are ideal. Services run between Vathy, Kioni, and smaller bays. Fares are usually affordable, and it's a convenient way to view the island from a new angle.

- **Practical Tips for Transportation Safety:** Always wear a seatbelt when driving or a helmet when cycling. Follow local speed limits and traffic signage. Mobile phone coverage in more rural places can be spotty, so notify someone of your travel plans and bring a printed map with you.
- **Language:** While many residents speak English, knowing a few Greek phrases can be useful. Simple words such as "efharisto" (thank you) and "parakalo" (please) are valued.
- **Navigation:** GPS tools like Google Maps work well on the island, but I found that having a thorough map of Ithaca was quite useful, especially when venturing off the usual route. Local tourist offices offer free maps, or you can purchase one from a bookstore.
- **Local Insights:** Do not be afraid to ask locals for directions or tips. Ithacans are extremely friendly and keen to provide information on hidden treasures and the best routes to travel.

Ithaca's transportation options may appear limited, but they contribute to the island's charm and adventure. Whether you're driving down coastal roads in a rental car, hiking a trail, or boating to quiet coves, the journey is part of the amazing Ithaca experience.

Chapter 7

LOCAL EXPLORATION AND ADVENTURE

Ithaca, Greece, is a hidden gem worth discovering, with breathtaking landscapes, beautiful blue oceans, and a rich cultural past. After spending so much time on this wonderful island, I've discovered a wealth of activities that promise both thrill and serenity. Let's look at the different methods you might explore and seek adventure in this wonderful region of the world.

Hiking Trails and Nature Walks

Ithaca is a hiker's dream, with routes winding through lush forests, historic ruins, and beautiful views. Here are some of my favorite treks and nature walks, which highlight the island's natural beauty and historical significance.

Anogi to Exogi Trail

This trail is a fantastic way to immerse yourself in Ithaca's diverse landscape. The trail begins at the town of Anogi, which is notable for its ancient monolithic stones and the Church of Panagia. It then travels through olive orchards and pastures. Along the walk, you will come across a number of historic ruins and little chapels. The trek goes to Exogi, a charming town positioned high on the northern tip of the island with panoramic views of the Ionian Sea.

Coordinates: Anogi (38.4581° N, 20.6789° E), Exogi (38.4715° N, 20.6615° E)

Roussano to Kathara Monastery

This walk combines history and environment. Starting in Roussano, a little village, you will trek up to the Kathara Monastery, which is located at one of the island's highest points. The track is well-marked and leads you through lush trees and rocky outcroppings. The monastery itself is a tranquil retreat with breathtaking views of the surrounding countryside.

Coordinates: Roussano (38.4206° N, 20.6763° E), Kathara Monastery (38.4423° N, 20.6827° E)

Neritos Forest

For a more leisurely walk, the Neritos Forest provides shaded walkways and pleasant natural noises. This forest is home to a diverse range of flora and wildlife, making it an ideal destination for nature enthusiasts and bird watchers. The forest trails are well-maintained and provide a serene escape from the more strenuous hikes.

Coordinates: Neritos Forest (38.4350° N, 20.6894° E

Sailing and Boating Adventures

Ithaca's coastline is filled with isolated coves, hidden beaches, and crystal-clear waters, making it a perfect location for sailors and boat owners. Here are some of the greatest ways to explore Ithaca by boat.

Sailing Around Ithaca

Chartering a sailboat is one of the most exciting ways to explore Ithaca. The island's numerous coves and inlets create calm waters ideal for sailing. Anchor at areas like Vathy, Kioni, and Frikes to discover each village's particular beauty. The calm winds and picturesque scenery make for a relaxed day on the lake.

Boat Rentals

If you want a more private experience, renting a small motorboat is an excellent choice. Several rental firms in Vathy and Kioni provide boats that do not require a license, allowing you to explore at your own pace. Popular destinations include Gidaki Beach, Filiatro Beach, and the Cave of the Nymphs, all of which offer hidden beauty and pure water.

Coordinates: Vathy (38.3681° N, 20.7155° E), Kioni (38.4587° N, 20.6879° E)

Kayaking Adventures

Kayaking along the shore of Ithaca is a gratifying experience for people who appreciate a little physical activity. Paddle across tranquil waters, find hidden caves, and visit beaches that can only be reached by sea. Guided kayaking trips are provided and provide information about the island's history and natural environment.

Snorkeling and diving spots

The undersea ecosystem surrounding Ithaca is as interesting as its landscapes. Snorkeling and diving are popular activities due to the beautiful, warm seas and diverse marine life.

Filiatro Beach

Filiatro Beach is a renowned snorkeling destination due to its clean waters and plentiful marine life. The beach is easily accessible and offers a moderate approach into the sea, making it ideal for beginners. You'll see colorful fish, sea urchins, and the rare octopus or two.

Coordinates: Filiatro Beach (38.3689° N, 20.7267° E)

Gidaki Beach

Gidaki Beach is one of the island's most stunning beaches and provides excellent snorkeling chances. The water here is extremely transparent, allowing you to observe the abundant marine life beneath. The beach is more isolated, resulting in fewer crowds and a more peaceful snorkeling experience.

Coordinates: Gidaki Beach (38.3614° N, 20.7231° E)

Diving in Polis Bay

Polis Bay is an excellent diving destination. The bay is famed for its underwater tunnels and diverse marine life. Several diving schools in Vathy and Stavros offer guided dives for all skill levels, including equipment and safety briefings. Exploring the underwater tunnels and seeing schools of fish, octopuses, and the occasional sea turtle is an unforgettable experience.

Coordinates: Polis Bay (38.4667° N, 20.6500° E)

Local Tours and Guided Excursions

Guided tours provide a better knowledge of Ithaca's rich history and natural beauty. There are tours available for anyone interested in mythology, history, or wildlife.

Historical and Mythological Tours

Ithaca is rich in mythological history, as Odysseus' fabled home. Several local guides give tours of key historical and mythological locations, including the Cave of the Nymphs and the Archaeological Museum of Vathy. These tours offer unique insights into the island's ancient history and importance in Greek mythology.

Coordinates: Cave of the Nymphs (38.4427° N, 20.6756° E), Archaeological Museum of Vathy (38.3676° N, 20.7161° E)

Nature and Wildlife Tours

Nature aficionados will enjoy guided tours of Ithaca's various landscapes. Explore the island's flora and animals, stop at protected areas, and learn about the efforts to conserve Ithaca's natural beauty. These tours frequently include visits to locations such as the Neritos Forest and the Anogi plateau.

Coordinates: Neritos Forest (38.4350° N, 20.6894° E), Anogi (38.4581° N, 20.6789° E)

Culinary Tours

A culinary tour allows you to immerse yourself in the local culture. These tours visit traditional taverns and local markets, giving you a taste of Ithaca's delectable cuisine. Learn about the island's culinary traditions, try local wines, and eat dishes cooked with fresh, local ingredients.

Coordinates: Vathy Market (38.3681° N, 20.7155° E), Kioni Tavernas (38.4587° N, 20.6879° E)

Practical Tips for Exploration

Exploring Ithaca involves some planning to ensure a seamless and pleasurable visit. Here are some practical suggestions based on my time on this lovely island.

- **Footwear and Clothing:** Comfortable footwear is vital, particularly if you intend to hike or stroll a lot. Lightweight, breathable clothes is ideal for

warm weather, but add a light jacket or sweater for chilly evenings. Don't forget your swimsuit and sun protection, which includes a hat and sunscreen.
- **Hydration and Snack:** Always bring a reusable water bottle to stay hydrated, especially on hikes and other outdoor activities. Local supermarkets have a range of snacks, but taking a few light snacks like almonds or fruit might be useful on lengthy trips.
- **Respect local customs:** Ithaca is a town where tradition and modernity coexist. When visiting religious locations, please respect local norms and dress modestly. Learning a few basic Greek phrases will help you show respect and connect with the locals.
- **Navigation:** While Ithaca is small, a decent map or a GPS-enabled device can help you navigate the city's twisting streets and paths. Local maps are accessible in tourist information centers, and many hotels also have them.

Conclusion

Ithaca, with its rich history, breathtaking scenery, and friendly residents, provides limitless options for exploration and adventure. From hiking through ancient ruins and sailing along the coast to snorkeling in crystal-clear waters and savoring local cuisine, every moment on this island is a chance to discover something new. Ithaca has something for everyone, whether you're a history buff, a nature lover, or just looking for a relaxing getaway. So pack your bags, put on your explorer's hat, and prepare to make wonderful experiences in this magical part of Greece.

Chapter 8

BUDGETING AND MONETARY TIPS

Daily Expense Estimates

Traveling to Ithaca can be a cost-effective adventure if you understand what to expect in terms of daily spending. During my stay there, I discovered that daily costs vary substantially based on your lifestyle and interests.

- **Accommodation:** You can find budget-friendly options like guesthouses and budget hotels ranging from €40-€70 per night. Mid-range accommodations, including boutique hotels, typically cost between €70 and €120 per night. Luxury resorts and villas can cost €150-€300 per night.
- **Food and Drink:** Eating out in Ithaca is both pleasurable and cost-effective. A lunch at a small taverna costs between €10 and €15, whilst a three-course meal at a mid-range restaurant costs between €25 and €40. If you enjoy

cooking, buying food is rather inexpensive, with a weekly grocery spend of €30-€50 per person.
- **Transportation:** Public transport is minimal, so renting a scooter (€20-€30 per day) or a car (€40-€60 per day) is common. Fuel costs roughly €1.70 per liter. Taxis are also available, but they can be more expensive for frequent use.
- **Activities:** Many of Ithaca's attractions are natural and free, like as beaches and hiking trails. Paid activities, such as boat rentals (€70-€150 per day) and guided tours (€20-€50 per person), enhance the whole experience while remaining affordable.
- **Miscellaneous:** Souvenirs, snacks, and other minor purchases can add up quickly, so budget between €10 and €20 each day for these.

In total, a comfortable daily budget for a mid-range traveler would be around €100-€150 per day, while budget travelers can manage on €60-€80 per day.

Money Saving Tips

Visiting Ithaca on a budget does not mean sacrificing experiences. Here are some tips that I found useful:

- **Travel Off-Season:** Visiting during the shoulder seasons (April-June and September-October) results in reduced accommodation costs and fewer crowds, making it simpler to find savings on flights and hotels.
- **Stay at Guesthouses:** Choose family-run guesthouses and pensions, which are not only cheaper but also provide a more genuine experience. Hosts frequently share useful local insights.
- **Cook Your Meals:** If your accommodation has a kitchenette, buy local produce and cook some of your meals. This saves money while allowing you to try fresh, local ingredients.
- **Use Public Transportation:** While limited, public busses are the most affordable method to get around. For short trips, consider walking or renting a bicycle.
- **Free Attractions:** Spend time enjoying Ithaca's natural beauties, including beaches, hiking trails, and overlooks, all of which are free to use.
- **Group Activities:** If you're traveling with friends or family, splitting the cost of accommodations, auto rentals, and boat cruises can help you save money.

Currency Exchange and Banking Services

If you're prepared, Ithaca's currency exchange and banking are simple:

- **Currency:** Greece uses the Euro (€). It's recommended to keep some euros on hand for little purchases and in isolated regions where credit cards may not be accepted.
- **ATMs:** ATMs are widely available in Vathy and other major villages. Be advised that some ATMs impose withdrawal fees, so check with your bank first. To save money on fees, withdraw larger sums.
- **Credit and Debit Cards:** Most restaurants, hotels, and shops accept credit and debit cards. However, smaller firms and markets may prefer cash, so have some on available.
- **Currency Exchange:** It is preferable to exchange your currency before arriving in Ithaca. If necessary, you can exchange money in banks in Vathy, however the rates may be less beneficial.
- **Banking Hours:** On weekdays, banks normally open from 8:00 a.m. until 2:30 p.m. They are

closed on weekends and public holidays, so plan accordingly for your banking needs.
- **Online Banking:** If your bank account permits online banking, consider transferring funds to a travel card that does not charge foreign transaction fees for ease and savings.

Shopping and Bargaining

Shopping in Ithaca is an enjoyable experience with numerous options to bring home unique souvenirs and gifts:

- **Local Markets:** Farmers' markets in Vathy and surrounding villages sell fresh produce, local cheeses, olive oil, and honey. These markets are ideal for purchasing high-quality, authentic products at affordable prices.
- **Souvenir Shops:** Look for shops that sell handmade crafts, ceramics, jewelry, and textiles. Popular items include embroidered linens, weaved baskets, and olive wood objects.
- **Bargaining Tips:** While bargaining is uncommon in most shops, it is permitted at markets and with street vendors. Approach bargaining politely and expect to pay a

reasonable price. A solid rule of thumb is to start with an offer that is 10-20% less than the asking price.
- **Specialty Shops:** Visit the local vineyards and distilleries to obtain high-quality local wines and spirits. Many offer samples and excursions, which enhance the experience.

Conclusion

Ithaca is a mesmerizing blend of natural beauty, rich history, and warm hospitality. With careful preparation and budgeting, you can fully enjoy everything this wonderful island has to offer without going overboard. Whether you're a frequent traveler or a first-time visitor, these tips and insights will help you navigate Ithaca and make the most of your stay. Enjoy every minute, and allow the island's charm to captivate your heart, as it has mine.

Chapter 9

SHOPPING AND ENTERTAINMENT IN ITHACA

As someone who has spent a lot of time discovering the nooks and corners of this beautiful island, I'm excited to give my tips on shopping and entertainment. Whether you're a first-time visitor, a seasoned traveler, or someone wishing to delve further into local culture, Ithaca has a rich tapestry of activities to keep you engaged and delighted. Let's dig in and discover the vibrant shopping scene and numerous entertainment alternatives that make Ithaca such a unique visit.

Local markets and souvenir shops

One of my favorite methods to get a sense of a city is to visit its markets. Ithaca has various local markets where you can buy everything from fresh produce to handcrafted items. The main market in Vathy, the island's capital, is a thriving hub where both locals and tourists come to shop, interact, and enjoy the lively environment.

- **Vathy Market:** Located near Vathy's major square, this market is a treasure trove of locally produced goods. Fresh fruits and vegetables are available, as well as locally made olive oil, honey, and a variety of herbs and spices. The merchants are pleasant and eager to give information about their items. Don't miss out on eating some local cheeses and freshly made bread; they're fantastic!
- **Kioni Village Shops:** Kioni, a picturesque village on the northeast coast, is home to several charming shops where you can find unique souvenirs. These stores provide a variety of products, including handcrafted jewelry and ceramics, as well as traditional Greek apparel and fabrics, that make ideal gifts or personal keepsakes. I also enjoy exploring the little art galleries that exhibit works by local artists; it's a terrific opportunity to bring a piece of Ithaca's creative energy home with you.
- **Filiatro Beach Kiosk:** If you're spending the day at Filiatro Beach, be sure to visit the beach kiosk. While it specializes on food and drinks, it also sells beach-themed souvenirs and locally manufactured crafts. It's a simple place to pick

up a souvenir from your beach day or a gift for someone back home.

Art galleries and cultural centers

Ithaca's vibrant cultural legacy is wonderfully shown in its art galleries and cultural institutes. These locations not only highlight the island's artistic skills, but also help visitors learn more about its history and traditions.

- **Anogi Cultural Center:** Located in the village of Anogi, this cultural center is a must-visit for anyone interested in Ithaca's history. The center presents a number of exhibitions and events commemorating the island's cultural past. From traditional music and dance performances to art exhibits and historical displays, there is always something intriguing going on here. I remember watching a folk dance performance here and being utterly captivated by the dancers' intensity and enthusiasm.
- **Vathy Art Gallery:** Located in the heart of Vathy, this gallery houses a broad collection of works by local and regional artists. The exhibits include contemporary paintings and sculptures,

as well as traditional crafts and photography. The gallery also conducts seminars and events, allowing visitors to connect with the local art community. One of the highlights for me was a pottery session, where I was able to create my own work of art.
- **Kioni Art Space:** Kioni's art space is a tiny but lively venue that exhibits the works of local artists. The gallery's shifting displays ensure that there is always something fresh to discover. During my visit, I was able to meet some of the artists and hear about their inspirations and creative processes. It was an extremely enlightening event that increased my admiration for Ithaca's artistic community.

Evening Entertainment & Events

When the sun goes down, Ithaca comes alive with a diverse range of entertainment options to suit all interests and inclinations. Whether you want to spend a calm evening with live music or dance the night away, there is something for everyone.

- **Live Music at Local Taverns:** Many of Ithaca's taverns and restaurants offer live music in the evenings. The melody of traditional Greek music fills the air as you eat a delicious meal and drink a glass of local wine. One of my favorite places is Taverna Kanenas in Vathy, where excellent local musicians frequently perform rebetiko, a type of Greek urban folk music. The ambiance is warm and welcoming, giving it the ideal location to unwind after a day of touring.

- **Outdoor Cinema in Vathy:** During the summer, Vathy holds outdoor cinema nights where you may see classic and current films under the stars. The films take place in an open-air theater near the port, which creates a magical setting for an evening of entertainment. I have pleasant memories of watching a movie here while taking in the gentle sea wind and the dazzling lights of town.
- **Local Festivals & Events:** Ithaca's calendar is jam-packed with festivals and events celebrating the island's culture and customs. The most notable is the Ithaca Arts Festival, which takes place every year in Vathy. The festival offers a variety of events, such as art exhibits, music performances, dance acts, and craft fairs. It's an excellent way to immerse yourself in the local culture and engage with the community. Another festival to visit is the Feast of Panagia, which is celebrated in several

communities with religious services, traditional music, and dance.

Shopping and Entertainment Tips:

To make the most of your shopping and entertainment experiences in Ithaca, here are a few suggestions based on my own experiences:

- **Shop Local:** When you buy handcrafted goods or locally manufactured items, you are supporting local artisans and companies. You'll not only get to keep a one-of-a-kind piece of Ithaca, but you'll also help the island's economy.
- **Ask for Recommendations:** Don't hesitate to ask locals for recommendations on where to shop and what events to attend. Ithacans are polite and proud of their culture, and they're always willing to offer their favorite sites and insider advice.
- **Plan Ahead:** Before your vacation, check the local events calendar to see if there are any festivals or special events scheduled for your stay. This allows you to arrange your itinerary and avoid missing out on any intriguing activities.

- **Embrace the Nightlife:** Ithaca's nightlife may not be as lively as that of larger cities, but it has its own appeal. Take some time to explore the local taverns, bars, and live music venues; you might come across a hidden treasure or meet new acquaintances.
- **Take it Slow:** Ithaca's shopping and entertainment are best appreciated at a relaxed pace. Take your time browsing the shops, chatting with sellers, and enjoying the activities. The island's laid-back vibe is contagious, and you'll find yourself slowing down and enjoying the small things.

Conclusion

Ithaca, with its rich cultural background, thriving art scene, and welcoming people, has a fantastic selection of shopping and entertainment alternatives. From lively markets and lovely souvenir shops to art galleries and live music venues, there is something for everyone's taste and interest. Immersing yourself in the local culture and embracing the island's distinctive attractions will allow you to build lasting memories and take home a piece of Ithaca's enchantment. Happy exploring!

Chapter 10
DINING AND NIGHTLIFE

Welcome to the culinary and nocturnal heart of Ithaca! I've spent a lot of time exploring the island's thriving culinary scene and nightlife, and I can tell you firsthand that Ithaca has an enticing blend of traditional Greek cuisine, cozy cafes, crowded bars, and energetic nightclubs. This chapter will take you through the island's top dining and nightlife experiences, ensuring that you enjoy every moment of your visit.

Traditional Greek cuisine

Ithaca's cuisine reflects the city's rich cultural background and abundance of natural resources. Traditional Greek food here focuses on fresh ingredients, uncomplicated preparations, and Mediterranean-inspired flavors. One of the first things I fell in love with was the meze, which is a collection of tiny dishes ideal for sharing. These are often served with a glass of ouzo or local wine.

Must-Try Dishes

- **Souvlaki:** Skewered and grilled meats, usually pork or chicken, served with pita bread, tomatoes, onions, and a dollop of tzatziki.
- **Moussaka**: A baked meal with layers of eggplant, minced meat, and béchamel sauce that is a comfort food staple.
- **Fasolada**: A hearty bean soup considered the national dish of Greece.
- **Kleftiko**: Slow-cooked lamb wrapped in parchment paper with herbs and vegetables.
- **Baklava**: A sweet pastry made of layers of filo filled with chopped nuts and honey.

I recall my first taste of moussaka in a modest family-run taverna in Vathy. The layers melted together, creating a symphony of flavors that was both foreign and familiar. This is the allure of Greek cuisine—the capacity to transport you to the land and its history with each bite.

Dining Etiquette:

- **Sharing is Caring:** Greek dinners are frequently communal, with numerous dishes distributed across the table.
- **Pace yourself:** Meals are leisurely affairs. Don't rush; instead, enjoy the procedure and company.

- **Compliments to the Chef:** If you enjoyed your meal, it's customary to complemen the chef. A simple "Efcharistó" (thank you) can go a long way.

Top Restaurants and Cafes

Ithaca is peppered with restaurants that appeal to a variety of tastes and interests. Here are a few of my top choices:

Top Restaurants:

- **O Batis (Vathy):** Situated directly on the waterfront, O Batis is a seafood lover's dream. The grilled octopus here is a must-try; it's delicate and tasty, and cooked to perfection.
- **Kohili (Frikes):** A small, charming restaurant known for its fresh fish and delightful meze. The view of the harbor enhances the overall experience.
- **Kanenas (Kioni):** Located in the lovely village of Kioni, this restaurant serves a blend of traditional and contemporary cuisine. The slow-cooked lamb kleftiko is amazing.

- **Rementzo (Frikes):** Known for its seafood platter and welcoming ambiance, Rementzo attracts both residents and tourists looking for a great supper.

Cozy cafes:

- **Spavento Bar (Kioni):** The ideal place for a morning coffee or an afternoon cocktail. Its easygoing atmosphere and breathtaking vistas make it a favorite among travelers.
- **Cafe Del Sol (Vathy):** This cafe, known for its delicious coffee and pastries, is perfect for a peaceful break while touring Vathy.
- **To Kentro (Stavros):** A popular site in the middle of Stavros that serves tasty snacks and is a terrific place to watch the world go by.

I recall spending many lazy afternoons at Spavento Bar, sipping an iced coffee and watching the boats sway softly in the port. These cafés are more than just places to dine; they are an important component of Ithaca's social fabric, where people share stories and create memories.

Popular Bars and Nightclubs

When the sun goes down, Ithaca's nightlife comes alive, with a mix of relaxed bars and vibrant nightclubs. Ithaca has something for everyone, whether you want to have a peaceful drink by the water or dance all night.

Best Bars:

- **Margarita Cafe Bar (Vathy):** A popular destination for both locals and tourists, recognized for its inventive drinks and lively environment. The live music performances here are a treat.
- **Sorokos Bar (Frikes):** Situated in the heart of Frikes, this bar is perfect for a relaxed evening. They make the best mojitos on the island.
- **Ithaki Garden (Vathy):** A lovely garden setting with a relaxing atmosphere, ideal for a romantic evening out.

Energetic Nightclubs:

- **Karamela Club (Vathy):** If you want to dance, here is the place to be. The music varies from Greek hits to worldwide dance tracks, so everyone has a fantastic time.
- **Araklis Club (Frikes):** Known for its themed nights and dynamic crowd, Araklis is the place

to let loose and fully experience the island's nightlife.

I recall one unforgettable night at Margarita Cafe Bar, when I ended up joining a group of locals in a spontaneous dance. The music, laughter, and friendship exemplified the Greek ethos of 'kefi' (joy).

Local Food Festivals & Events

Ithaca celebrates its culinary legacy through a variety of food festivals and events held throughout the year. These festivals are excellent opportunities to immerse oneself in local culture while also enjoying amazing food.

- **Ithaca Gastronomy Festival:**

When: Usually held in late summer.

Where: Vathy.

A celebration of Ithaca's culinary traditions, featuring cooking demonstrations, food stalls, and tastings. Local cooks demonstrate their skills, and visitors may enjoy anything from fresh fish to traditional pastries.

- **Wine festivals:**

When: Various dates throughout the year.

Where: Different villages across the island.

These celebrations honor the local winemaking traditions. You'll have the opportunity to sample a range of local wines and learn about the winemaking process.

- **Fisherman's Festival:**

When: August

Where: Frikes.

A lively festival that celebrates the island's fishing heritage. Expect lots of fresh seafood, music, and dancing.

The Ithaca Gastronomy Festival was a highlight of my trip. The perfume of freshly cooked food floating through the air, the cheery banter of locals and guests, and the pure thrill of discovering new sensations all contributed to an unforgettable experience.

Conclusion

Dining and nightlife in Ithaca provide a diverse range of experiences, from traditional Greek cuisine to a boisterous night out. The island's restaurants and bars are more than just places to dine and drink; they are windows into Ithaca's character, each with its own personality and narrative. Whether you're a foodie, a night owl, or just someone who enjoys exploring different cultures, Ithaca will leave you with amazing experiences and a desire to return.

Chapter 11

ACCOMMODATION OPTIONS

When visiting Ithaca, Greece, you can discover a variety of accommodation options to suit all types of travelers. Ithaca has something for everyone, whether you want luxurious resorts with spectacular views, budget hotels, quaint boutique guesthouses, or unique accommodations. From the moment you arrive on this wonderful island, the warmth and kindness of the islanders will make you feel right at home.

Luxury resorts

Ithaca's luxury resorts offer an unmatched experience for those looking to indulge. Imagine waking up to spectacular views of the Ionian Sea, eating a delicious breakfast on a sun-kissed balcony, and spending your days lazing by infinity pools or relaxing in cutting-edge spas. Some of the top luxury resorts are:

- **Perantzada Art Hotel** - Located in Vathy, this hotel combines modern art with classic luxury. The rooms are individually adorned with contemporary artworks, and the views of the bay are breathtaking.
- **Cavos Inn** - Located in Kioni, Cavos Inn provides a peaceful escape with tastefully constructed accommodations and exceptional service. The infinity pool, which overlooks the bay, is a highlight.
- **Stavros Hotel** - Located in the heart of Stavros, this hotel offers luxury rooms with private balconies, an exceptional restaurant, and a wellness center for relaxation.

These resorts not only provide high-quality amenities, but also personalized services to ensure a wonderful stay. From arranging private boat tours to planning gourmet dinners beneath the stars, the staff goes above and beyond to make your stay memorable.

Budget-Friendly Hotels

Traveling on a budget should not imply sacrificing comfort or pleasure. There are some budget-friendly hotels in Ithaca that provide excellent value.

These hotels offer clean, pleasant accommodations along with necessary conveniences. Some popular alternatives are:

- **Mentor Hotel** - Located in Vathy, Mentor Hotel is known for its friendly staff and convenient location. The accommodations are basic but well-maintained, and the views of the bay are stunning.
- **Lazaretto Palace** - This Kioni hotel offers cheap rooms with stunning sea views. The atmosphere is pleasant, and the staff is always willing to assist with any inquiries.
- **Nostos Hotel** - Located in Frikes, Nostos Hotel offers a pleasant atmosphere with a classic Greek feel. The accommodations are comfortable, and being close to the beach is a benefit.

Staying at budget-friendly hotels allows you to save money while still experiencing Ithaca's beauty and charm. These hotels frequently offer a more authentic experience, allowing you to interact with locals and explore the island like a resident.

Boutique guesthouses

Staying at one of Ithaca's boutique guesthouses provides a more intimate and customized experience. These guesthouses typically offer fewer rooms, allowing for greater attention to detail and a more welcoming ambiance. Some outstanding options are:

- **Villa Olga** - Located in Vathy, Villa Olga offers a charming and cozy setting with beautifully decorated rooms and a lovely garden. The hosts are well-known for their warm hospitality and tasty prepared breakfasts.
- **Korina Gallery Hotel** - This boutique guesthouse in Vathy combines traditional architecture with modern comforts. The rooms are tastefully decorated, and the rooftop terrace is an ideal place to unwind and take in the views.
- **Rhapsody Apartments** - Located in Kioni, Rhapsody Apartments provides spacious and well-appointed rooms with spectacular sea views. The tranquil surroundings and courteous hosts make it an excellent choice for a relaxed holiday.

Staying in a boutique guesthouse offers a unique opportunity to immerse yourself in local culture while also receiving customized attention that larger hotels frequently do not. These accommodations are ideal for guests who want a more casual and authentic experience.

Unique Stays

If you're looking for something genuinely unique, Ithaca has various options that promise an unforgettable encounter. These accommodations go beyond the standard hotel room, with unique amenities and locations. Some of the most fascinating options are:

- **Cave Houses** - For a memorable experience, consider renting a cave house. These traditional homes, cut into the hillside, provide a unique combination of history and comfort. They keep cool in the summer and give a pleasant sanctuary in the winter.
- **Stone Villas** - Scattered throughout the island, stone villas provide a rustic but elegant experience. These homes frequently come with

private pools, beautiful gardens, and breathtaking views of the surrounding area.
- **Sailboat Accommodations** - For the ultimate maritime adventure, stay on a sailboat docked in one of Ithaca's picturesque ports. These accommodations offer a unique view of the island and allow you to explore the coastline at your leisure.

A unique stay allows you to see Ithaca in a way that regular accommodations cannot. These unique options, whether you're living in a cave house, a stone villa, or a sailboat, bring an added element of adventure to your trip.

Top Recommended Accommodation

With so many options, it might be difficult to choose where to stay. Here are a few top recommendations based on my personal experiences and input from other travelers:

- **Perantzada Art Hotel (Vathy):** Luxurious and artistic, with breathtaking views and excellent service.

- **Mentor Hotel (Vathy):** Affordable, strategically located, and comfortable.
- **Kioni Village Guesthouse (Kioni)** is intimate and attractive, with a friendly atmosphere.
- **Stone House (Perachori):** A classic Greek experience that is authentic and unique.
- **Windmill House (Anogi):** Historical and magnificent, with stunning views.

Choosing the Right Accommodation for You

Choosing the appropriate accommodation is determined by your personal tastes and budget. Here are a few suggestions to help you decide:

- **Consider Your Budget:** Determine how much you are willing to spend on accommodation. Luxury resorts provide excellent amenities, but at a premium cost. Budget hotels and guesthouses offer comfort without breaking the wallet.
- **Think about location:** Choose whether you wish to stay in a busy town like Vathy, a picturesque village like Kioni, or a peaceful

location like Perachori. Consider the vicinity of attractions, restaurants, and transportation.
- **Look for Amenities:** Determine whatever amenities are important to you. Do you want a pool, a spa, or cooking facilities? Make certain that your chosen accommodation suits your requirements.
- **Read reviews:** Check out reviews from other travelers to get a sense of the quality and service. Websites such as TripAdvisor and Booking.com provide excellent opportunities for honest reviews.
- **Consider the Experience**: Think about the type of experience you want. Would you rather stay in a magnificent resort, a cozy guesthouse, or somewhere unique? Choose accommodation that suits your travel style.

Booking Tips and Tricks

Here are some booking suggestions to help you get the greatest deals and reserve your desired accommodation.

- **Book Early:** Ithaca is a popular destination, especially during the high season. To minimize

disappointment, book your accommodations well in advance.
- **Use booking platforms:** Websites such as Booking.com, Airbnb, and Expedia provide a variety of options and frequently offer exceptional deals.
- **Check for Discounts:** Look for discounts and specials. Many hotels and guesthouses offer discounts for extended stays or off-season bookings.
- **Contact the property directly:** Sometimes you might receive better deals by calling the accommodation directly. They may provide exclusive bargains that are not available on booking portals.
- **Read the fine print:** Before booking, ensure that you understand the cancellation policy, check-in/out hours, and any additional fees.

Booking Platforms

When planning your stay in Ithaca, consider the following popular booking platforms:

- **Booking.com:** Offers a wide range of accommodation options, from luxury resorts to

budget hotels and guesthouses. It is easy to use and offers extensive reviews and ratings.
- **Airbnb:** Great for unique stays and home-like experiences. You may discover everything from traditional homes to modern apartments.
- **Expedia:** A comprehensive travel site that offers accommodation, flights, and car rentals. It is convenient to book multiple travel services in one spot.
- **Hotels.com:** Specializes in hotel bookings and often has exclusive deals and discounts. It's an excellent alternative for discovering budget-friendly accommodations.
- **TripAdvisor:** Offers reviews and ratings from other travelers, making it easier to find the ideal accommodation. It also provides booking services.

Ithaca is a beautiful place to stay, with many of options to satisfy every tourist. Whether you're looking for luxury, comfort, or something unique, you'll discover the ideal location to call home during your visit. Enjoy the warm welcome, breathtaking views, and charming atmosphere that make Ithaca a really unique destination.

Chapter 12

WHAT TO DO AND NOT TO DO

Respecting Local Culture

When strolling the picturesque trails of Ithaca, Greece, it's important to appreciate and enjoy the local culture. Ithacans, like many Greeks, are proud of their heritage, and respecting their traditions will go a long way toward making your vacation enjoyable and enriching.

- **Dress modestly:** While Ithaca is generally laid-back, modest dress is preferred, especially while visiting religious places such as the Kathara Monastery or the Panagia Church in Anogi. Ladies, a light scarf to protect your shoulders in these areas is a nice option. Gentlemen, it is courteous to avoid extremely informal apparel, such as swimwear, away from the beach.
- **Greetings & Social Etiquette:** Greeks are warm and welcoming. A friendly "Kalimera" (Good morning) or "Kalispera" (Good evening) will be

warmly welcomed. In more official circumstances, a simple nod or handshake is suitable. Keep in mind that personal space may be less than you are accustomed to; this is a symbol of friendship and connection.
- **Dining Etiquette:** Dining in Ithaca is a social activity. It is customary to share meals, so don't be shocked if your Greek host or new local acquaintance offers you a taste from their plate. When dining out, it is customary to offer a little tip for good service, usually around 10%.
- **Religious Observance:** Respecting religious customs is important. If you chance to be in Ithaca during a religious event, please participate appropriately. In churches, speak gently, dress appropriately, and avoid taking photos unless explicitly permitted.
- **Punctuality and Time:** Greeks take a more relaxed approach to time. Don't be surprised if things don't start as planned. Embrace the slower, more meditative rhythm of island life.

Environmental considerations

Ithaca's natural beauty is one of its most appealing aspects, and conserving it is critical. Here are some ways you may help improve the island's environmental health.

- **Waste Disposal:** Always dispose of waste appropriately. Many sites, particularly beaches and hiking routes, have dumpsters. If you're going somewhere distant, bring a little bag to store any rubbish.
- **Reduce Plastic Use:** Single-use plastics are a major global issue. Choose reusable water bottles, and for picnics, use biodegradable or reusable containers. Many local cafés and restaurants will happily fill your bottle with tap water, which is normally safe to drink.
- **Respect Wildlife:** Ithaca is home to a variety of wildlife species. While it is enjoyable to encounter animals on your trips, keep a respectful distance. Avoid feeding wild animals since it can upset their natural routines and health.
- **Stay on routes:** When hiking or exploring, stick to marked routes to avoid harm to plants and erosion. This is especially crucial in sensitive locations like the Mount Neritos region.
- **Water Conservation:** Water is a valuable resource on islands. Take shorter showers, reuse towels, and conserve water whenever feasible. Many motels have installed water-

saving measures, and your assistance is greatly appreciated.

Safety Tips for Tourists

Staying safe in Ithaca will make your visit memorable for all the right reasons. Here are some useful suggestions to keep in mind.

- **Personal Safety:** Ithaca is generally relatively safe, with a low crime rate. However, it is always wise to use common sense. Keep a watch on your stuff, especially in crowded areas such as Vathy's shoreline. Use hotel safes to store valuables.
- **Swimming Safety:** Ithaca's crystal-clear waters are enticing, but only swim in permitted places. Pay heed to local currents and avoid swimming alone. If you're not an experienced swimmer, stay on beaches with lifeguards, such as Filiatro Beach.
- **Hiking and Outdoor Safety:** The island's rocky landscape is ideal for hiking. Wear adequate footwear, bring a map, and notify someone of your plans if you are going out alone. Bring

enough water and be ready for rapid weather changes, especially in hilly locations.
- **Health Precautions**: While there are no mandated vaccines in Greece, it is a good idea to have your routine immunizations up to date. Carry a modest first-aid kit to treat minor injuries. Pharmacies are well-stocked, and pharmacists typically speak fluent English.
- **Emergency Contacts**: Keep a note of emergency numbers. The general emergency number in Greece is 112, but particular services such as police (100), fire department (199), and medical emergencies (166) are also accessible.

CONCLUSION AND FAREWELL

As our tour through the wonderful island of Ithaca comes to a close, I hope this guide piqued your interest and provided useful information for your stay. Ithaca, with its rich history, stunning landscapes, and friendly people, provides a unique combination of adventure and relaxation. Ithaca offers a memorable experience, whether you're tracing Odysseus' footsteps, discovering the island's hidden beauties, or simply relaxing on its beaches and villages.

Embrace the local spirit

Remember that Ithaca's magic rests not only in its natural beauty, but also in its cultural depth and people's character. Respecting local customs, maintaining the environment, and participating with the community will allow you to contribute to the island's well-being while enjoying your journey. Every grin, "Kalimera," and shared meal contributes to the tapestry of memories you will make here.

Practical Tips Recap

Stay careful, plan ahead, and enjoy the island's slower pace. Make sure you have your emergency contacts on hand, follow local customs, and stay aware of your surroundings. Use this guide to get started, but allow curiosity and spontaneity lead your excursions.

Parting Thoughts

As I bid you farewell, I leave you with this thought: travel is about more than just seeing new places; it is about truly experiencing them, grasping their essence, and allowing them to influence you. Ithaca, with its fabled appeal and ageless charm, is a destination that lingers long after you leave its shores.

Whether you're here for the first time or returning for another journey, May Ithaca inspire, challenge, and fill your heart with wonderful experiences. Safe travels, and may your trip be as memorable as the island itself.

Farewell

Thank you for letting me be your guide in Ithaca. I hope you find this information useful and enhances your vacation experience. Remember that the world is full of wonders waiting to be discovered, and Ithaca is just one of many treasures. Farewell, and may your journey be one of joy, discovery, and limitless inspiration. Until we meet again, happy exploring!

APPENDIX: USEFUL RESOURCES

Emergency Contacts and Contact Information

General Emergency Number

- EU Emergency Number (Police, Fire, Ambulance): 112
- Police
- Local Police Station in Vathy: +30 26740 32205
- Tourist Police: +30 26740 32205

Medical Services

- Local Medical Center in Vathy: +30 26740 32222
- Vathy Medical Center Emergency Line: +30 26740 32411
- Hospital in Argostoli (Kefalonia): +30 26710 28201

Fire Department

- Fire Department in Vathy: +30 26740 32224
- Forest Fire Reporting: +30 199

Coast Guard and Marine Services

- Port Authority in Vathy: +30 26740 32909

- Port Authority in Piso Aetos: +30 26740 31920
- Kefalonia Port Authority (for ferry connections): +30 26710 22224

Pharmacies

- Vathy Pharmacy: +30 26740 32208
- Stavros Pharmacy: +30 26740 31448
- Kioni Pharmacy: +30 26740 31454

Taxi Services

- Vathy Taxi Service: +30 26740 32555
- Stavros Taxi Service: +30 26740 31125

Tourist Information

- Tourist Information Office in Vathy: +30 26740 32980
- Tourist Information Office in Kioni: +30 26740 31200

Embassy and Consulate Contacts

- British Embassy in Athens: +30 210 7272 600
- U.S. Embassy in Athens: +30 210 721 2951
- Canadian Embassy in Athens: +30 210 727 3400
- Australian Embassy in Athens: +30 210 870 4000

Vehicle Assistance

- Roadside Assistance (ELPA): +30 10400
- Europ Assistance Greece: +30 210 349 0190

- Interamerican Road Assistance: +30 210 946 2000

Travel and Tourism Services

- Ithaca Travel Agency: +30 26740 33151
- Ionian Ferries (Ferry Services): +30 26740 33570
- Kefalonian Lines (Ferry Services): +30 26710 25110

Local Government Offices

- Municipality of Ithaca: +30 26740 32900
- Citizen Service Center (KEP) in Vathy: +30 26740 33120

Maps and Navigational Tools

Navigating Ithaca is relatively straightforward, but having a good map or navigational tool can enhance your experience. There are several useful maps and apps to consider:

- **Google Maps:** Always reliable, and you can download the map for offline use.
- **Maps.me:** This is another great app that offers detailed offline maps, which can be very handy

given the island's sometimes spotty internet coverage.
- **Local Tourist Maps:** These are available at the port, in most hotels, and tourist information centers. They often highlight hiking trails, points of interest, and local businesses.

I personally found using a combination of Google Maps and local tourist maps to be the most effective. The local maps provided me with insight into lesser-known spots that weren't always highlighted on Google.

Additional Reading and References

For those who love to delve deeper into the history and culture of a place, Ithaca offers a rich tapestry of literature:

- **"The Odyssey" by Homer:** An obvious choice, this epic poem is centered around the legendary Greek hero Odysseus and his long journey back home to Ithaca.
- **"Travels in Greece" by Richard Chandler**: This book provides an in-depth historical and

archaeological perspective on Greece, including Ithaca.
- **"Greek Islands" by Lawrence Durrell:** Durrell's work captures the essence of the Greek islands, with beautiful prose and vivid descriptions.
- **Local Guides:** There are several locally published guidebooks available in Vathy that offer detailed insights into hiking trails, local flora and fauna, and historical sites.

Useful Local Phrases

Even though most people in Ithaca speak English, learning a few Greek phrases can enhance your experience and show respect for the local culture. Here are some basics:

General Greetings and Politeness
- Good morning: Καλημέρα (Kalimera)
- Good evening: Καλησπέρα (Kalispera)
- Good night: Καληνύχτα (Kalinikhta)
- Welcome: Καλώς ήρθατε (Kalos irthate)
- How are you?: Πώς είσαι; (Pos ise?)
- Fine, thank you: Καλά, ευχαριστώ (Kala, efharisto)

- Excuse me / Sorry: Συγγνώμη (Signomi)

In Restaurants and Cafes

- I would like...: Θα ήθελα... (Tha ithela...)
- Menu: Μενού (Menu)
- What do you recommend?: Τι προτείνετε; (Ti protinete?)
- Check, please: Τον λογαριασμό, παρακαλώ (Ton logariasmo, parakalo)
- Delicious: Νόστιμο (Nostimo)
- I am vegetarian: Είμαι χορτοφάγος (Ime hortofagos)
- Is this spicy?: Είναι αυτό πικάντικο; (Ine afto pikantiko?)
- Without...: Χωρίς... (Horis...)
- Water: Νερό (Nero)
- Wine: Κρασί (Krasi)

Shopping and Markets

- How much is this?: Πόσο κάνει αυτό; (Poso kani afto?)
- Can I try this on?: Μπορώ να το δοκιμάσω; (Boro na to dokimaso?)
- Do you have this in another color/size?: Το έχετε αυτό σε άλλο χρώμα/μέγεθος; (To echete afto se allo chroma/megethos?)
- Where can I find...?: Πού μπορώ να βρω...? (Pou boro na vro...?)
- I am just looking: Απλά κοιτάζω (Apla kitazo)

- Can you give me a discount?: Μπορείτε να μου κάνετε έκπτωση; (Mporite na mou kanete ekptosi?)

Directions and Transportation

- Where is...?: Πού είναι...? (Pou ine...?)
- How do I get to...?: Πώς πάω στο/στη...? (Pos pao sto/sti...?)
- Left: Αριστερά (Aristera)
- Right: Δεξιά (Deksia)
- Straight ahead: Ευθεία (Eftheia)
- Near: Κοντά (Konda)
- Far: Μακριά (Makria)
- Bus stop: Στάση λεωφορείου (Stasi leoforiou)
- Taxi: Ταξί (Taksi)
- Train station: Σταθμός τρένου (Stathmos trenou)

Accommodation

- Do you have any rooms available?: Έχετε δωμάτια διαθέσιμα; (Echete domatia diathesima?)
- I have a reservation: Έχω μια κράτηση (Echo mia kratisi)
- What time is breakfast?: Τι ώρα είναι το πρωινό; (Ti ora ine to proino?)
- Can I have an extra blanket/pillow?: Μπορώ να έχω μια επιπλέον κουβέρτα/μαξιλάρι; (Boro na echo mia epipleon kuverta/maxilari?)
- Check-in: Εγγραφή (Engrafi)

- Check-out: Αναχώρηση (Anahorisi)

Health and Safety

- I need a doctor: Χρειάζομαι γιατρό (Chriazome yatro)
- Pharmacy: Φαρμακείο (Farmakio)
- I am allergic to...: Είμαι αλλεργικός/ή σε... (Ime allergikos/í se...)
- Help!: Βοήθεια! (Voitheia!)
- Call the police: Καλέστε την αστυνομία (Kaleste tin astynomia)
- I am lost: Έχω χαθεί (Echo hathei)
- Emergency: Έκτακτη ανάγκη (Ektakti anangi)

Social and Cultural

- What is your name?: Πώς σε λένε; (Pos se lene?)
- My name is...: Με λένε... (Me lene...)
- Where are you from?: Από πού είσαι; (Apo pou ise?)
- I am from...: Είμαι από... (Ime apo...)
- Nice to meet you: Χάρηκα που σε γνώρισα (Harika pou se gnorisa)
- Happy holidays: Καλές γιορτές (Kales yiortes)
- Congratulations: Συγχαρητήρια (Synharitiria)

Using these phrases can be particularly useful in more remote areas or when interacting with older locals who may not speak English as fluently.

Addresses and Locations of Popular Accommodation

Finding the right place to stay can make or break your trip. Here are some of the most popular accommodations on the island:

Perantzada Art Hotel

- Address: Odos Pinelopis, Vathy 283 00, Greece
- Coordinates: 38.3680° N, 20.7208° E

Korina Gallery Hotel

- Address: Tsamadou 3, Vathy 283 00, Greece
- Coordinates: 38.3676° N, 20.7211° E

Ithaca's Poem

- Address: Odos Odyssea Androutsou, Vathy 283 00, Greece
- Coordinates: 38.3691° N, 20.7188° E

Familia Hotel

- Address: Tsirigoti 3, Vathy 283 00, Greece
- Coordinates: 38.3678° N, 20.7213° E

These hotels offer a range of amenities and are centrally located, making them convenient for exploring the island.

Addresses and Locations of Popular Restaurants and Cafes

Ithaca has a vibrant food scene, from traditional tavernas to chic cafes. Here are some top picks:

O Batis Restaurant

- Address: Vathy Waterfront, Vathy 283 00, Greece
- Coordinates: 38.3668° N, 20.7222° E

Libretto Trattoria

- Address: Central Square, Vathy 283 00, Greece
- Coordinates: 38.3671° N, 20.7203° E

Ageri Restaurant

- Address: Odos Odyssea Androutsou, Vathy 283 00, Greece
- Coordinates: 38.3694° N, 20.7184° E

Cafe Spavento

- Address: Kioni Waterfront, Kioni 283 00, Greece
- Coordinates: 38.4477° N, 20.7128° E

These establishments offer a variety of dining experiences, from traditional Greek cuisine to international dishes, and are perfect for enjoying a meal with a view.

Addresses and Locations of Popular Bars and Clubs

For those looking to enjoy the nightlife, Ithaca has several lively spots:

Spathis Bar

- Address: Vathy Harbor, Vathy 283 00, Greece
- Coordinates: 38.3672° N, 20.7219° E

Sorokos Bar

- Address: Kioni Waterfront, Kioni 283 00, Greece
- Coordinates: 38.4475° N, 20.7129° E

Cantina Bar

- Address: Vathy Waterfront, Vathy 283 00, Greece
- Coordinates: 38.3669° N, 20.7221° E

Drosia Bar

- Address: Platrithias, Ithaca 283 00, Greece
- Coordinates: 38.4531° N, 20.6924° E

These bars offer a mix of music, drinks, and great company, perfect for a night out.

Addresses and Locations of Book Shops

For those who love to read, there are several cozy bookshops on the island:

Ithaca Books

- Address: Odos Odyssea Androutsou, Vathy 283 00, Greece
- Coordinates: 38.3692° N, 20.7187° E

Anemone Bookstore

- Address: Central Square, Vathy 283 00, Greece
- Coordinates: 38.3674° N, 20.7205° E

Bookstore Kioni

- Address: Kioni Village, Kioni 283 00, Greece
- Coordinates: 38.4478° N, 20.7130° E

These shops offer a range of books, including travel guides, novels, and historical texts about Ithaca.

Addresses and Locations of Top Clinics, Hospitals, and Pharmacies

Healthcare facilities on the island ensure you can access medical help if needed:

Vathy Medical Center

- Address: Vathy 283 00, Greece
- Coordinates: 38.3680° N, 20.7206° E

Vathy Pharmacy

- Address: Central Square, Vathy 283 00, Greece
- Coordinates: 38.3671° N, 20.7202° E

Pharmacy Kioni

- Address: Kioni Village, Kioni 283 00, Greece
- Coordinates: 38.4476° N, 20.7129° E

Stavros Clinic

- Address: Stavros 283 00, Greece
- Coordinates: 38.4420° N, 20.6931° E

These facilities are well-equipped to handle a range of medical needs, ensuring you have peace of mind during your stay.

Addresses and Locations of UNESCO World Heritage Sites

While Ithaca itself doesn't host any UNESCO World Heritage Sites, nearby Kefalonia does:

Drogarati Cave, Kefalonia

- Address: Chaliotata, Kefalonia 280 80, Greece
- Coordinates: 38.1889° N, 20.5658° E

Melissani Cave, Kefalonia

- Address: Karavomylos, Kefalonia 280 80, Greece
- Coordinates: 38.2503° N, 20.6039° E

Both sites are accessible via a short ferry ride from Ithaca, offering stunning natural beauty and historical significance.

Photo or image attribution

https://www.greeka.com/photos/ionian/ithaca/sightseeing/hero/ithaca-sightseeing-1280.webp

https://www.greeka.com/village_beach/photos/42/vathy-top-1-1280.webp

https://images.greeka.com/resized/user_images/greeka/580/phpnsM4nM.jpeg

https://www.greeka.com/village_beach/photos/1285/stavros-gallery-2-480.jpg

https://www.ithaca.gr/wp-content/uploads/1-%CE%9A%CE%95%CE%99%CE%9C%CE%95%CE%9D%CE%9F-%C2%A9-%CE%91lexandra-Varvarigou-DSCN2881.jpg

https://images.greeka.com/resized/user_images/fede2016/580/migEdgKeL.jpeg

https://images.greeka.com/resized/user_images/fede2016/580/migxbBwaj.jpeg

https://www.greeka.com/seedo/photos/1094/ithaca-ancient-town-of-alalcomenae-top-1-1280.webp

https://www.greeka.com/seedo/photos/568/ithaca-church-of-savior-christ-top-1-1280.webp

Conclusion

The appendix of this guide serves as a comprehensive resource for anyone traveling to Ithaca, Greece. From emergency contacts to the best bookshops, this information will help ensure your trip is safe, enjoyable, and thoroughly enriching. Whether you're a first-time visitor or returning to explore more of what this beautiful island has to offer, having detailed, practical information at your fingertips can make all the difference.

MAPS

SCAN HERE TO GO DIRECTLY TO THE MAP

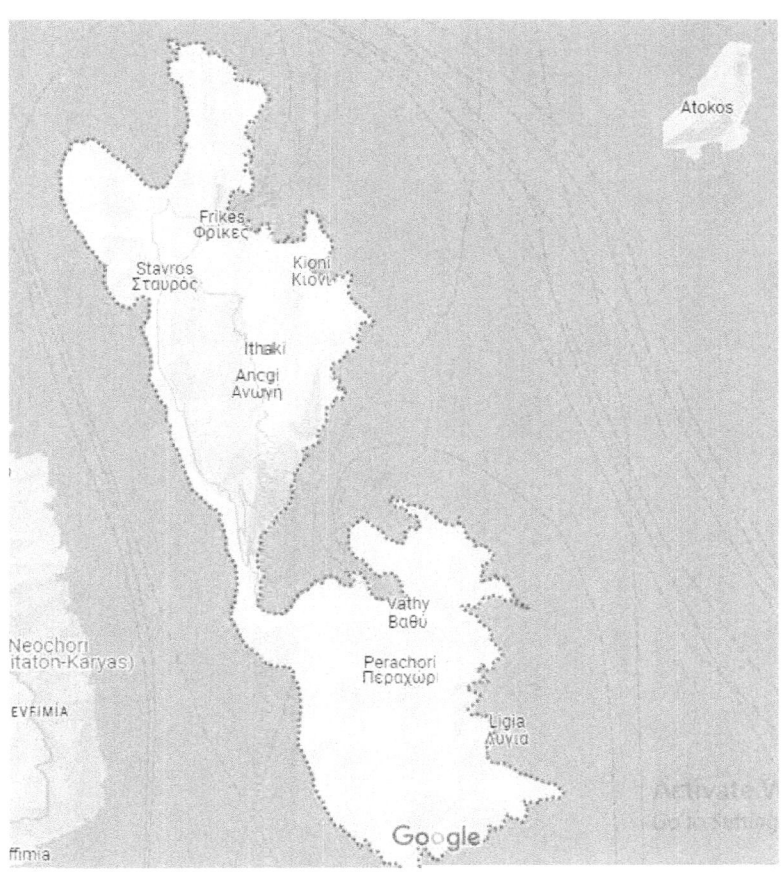

https://maps.app.goo.gl/vruCSRnxoEYSD7Wr9

Things to do:
https://maps.app.goo.gl/icHFd2hnD9RUpPRXA

Restaurants:
https://maps.app.goo.gl/s1W6CEPhhxPryatM6

Banks:
https://maps.app.goo.gl/fgXp75THRuWfxScs7

Printed in Dunstable, United Kingdom

6775343838R00107